"Our republic is the greatest creation of mankind, but there is no guarantee it will continue to be. Sebastian Gorka has done us a major service by mapping the threats America faces and providing a plan to defeat them. In *Why We Fight*, he also gives us a timely reminder of what it means to be a hero and what it means to defend America. In addition to his innate wisdom, Gorka has the unique insight resulting from his family's experience with real evil. In general, those who have experienced evil appreciate good more than those who have not. In other words, unlike most of our intellectuals today, Sebastian Gorka is not naïve. Another reason to read this important book."

> **—DENNIS PRAGER**, nationally syndicated radio talk show host and author of nine books, including the national bestseller *The Rational Bible*, and founder of the internet-based Prager University

"Sebastian Gorka gets President Trump. And he gets national security. In *Defeating Jihad*, he showed us how to take down the terrorists. Now with *Why We Fight*, he uses his experience as strategist to the president to give us the plan to deal with our other enemies. Read this book. Buy it for your friends and relatives."

> **—JUDGE JEANINE PIRRO**, host of *Justice with Judge Jeanine* and author of *Liars, Leakers, and Liberals*

"America stands for liberty and as a result, we will always have enemies. Sebastian Gorka's *Why We Fight* gives us the plan to defeat them and keep our republic safe while sharing the stirring stories of some of our nation's greatest heroes. If you believe in 'America First!' this is your book."

> **—MARK LEVIN**, host of the *Mark Levin Show* and author of *Rediscovering Americanism*

"With Donald Trump as president, America is back, and we are Making America Great Again. Dr. Gorka is one of the most important MAGA voices we have, and in *Why We Fight*, he shows us what it will take to defeat our enemies and just why America is so special. Buy it. Read it. And spread the word."

> **—SEAN HANNITY**, host of *The Sean Hannity Show* and author of three books, including the national bestsellers *Conservative Victory* and *Deliver Us from Evil*

"Why has America often become mired in inconclusive, post-war unconventional conflicts? In a study, historical analysis, critique of military analysts, and memoir as a former Trump administration security advisor, Sebastian Gorka persuasively argues that the absence of willpower, unity, common sense, and political and moral clarity is usually the culprit—not just the inherent dangers of the nuclear age or asymmetrical warfare. An accessible, inspiring, and needed discussion of a classic American dilemma."

> **—VICTOR DAVIS HANSON**, Senior Fellow at the Hoover Institution and author of *The Second World Wars*

"Donald Trump is fearlessly restoring the America of our Founding Fathers and making all Americans safe again. Sebastian Gorka was his strategist. Dr. Gorka knows Donald Trump and the threats we face. Buy and read *Why We Fight* to find how we win and what it means to be an American hero."

> **—RUSH LIMBAUGH**, radio talk show host of *The Rush Limbaugh Show* and bestselling author of the *Rush Revere* series

"Sebastian Gorka understands my father, the significance of the historic November 8, 2016 election, and the power of the Make America Great Again movement. *Why We Fight* provides deep insight into the threats America faces and how to keep our country strong. Under President Trump, America is back!"

> **—ERIC TRUMP**, Executive Vice President of The Trump Organization

WHY WE FIGHT

SEBASTIAN GORKA

Why We Fight

DEFEATING AMERICA'S ENEMIES —WITH NO APOLOGIES

REGNERY
PUBLISHING
A Division of Salem Media Group

Regnery® is a registered trademark of Salem Communications Holding Corporation

Cataloging-in-Publication data on file with the Library of Congress

ISBN 978-1-62157-640-2
ebook ISBN 978-1-62157-695-2

Published in the United States by
Regnery Publishing
A Division of Salem Media Group
300 New Jersey Ave NW
Washington, DC 20001
www.Regnery.com

Manufactured in the United States of America

10 9 8 7 6 5 4 3 2 1

Books are available in quantity for promotional or premium use. For information on discounts and terms, please visit our website: www.Regnery.com.

To Katie, Paul, and Julia, who never lose faith in dad.

And to all those friends who stand up for the truth when it is not politically correct to do so.

Thank you:
Bruce Abramson, Jeff Ballabon, Omri Ceren, David Goldman, Ira Greenstein, Paul Packer, Judge Jeanine Pirro, Dennis Prager, Sean Hannity, Mort Klein, Liel Leibovitz, Mark Levin, Tibor Navracsics, Katie Pavlich, David Reaboi, Arthur Schwartz, Mark Steyn, and Rabbi Hershel Billet.

Contents

What It Means to Be a Freedom Fighter

*T*he cell was cold. In the winter the only warmth came from the bodies of prisoners crammed into a tiny space designed for just two inmates, but under the new regime, housed up to a dozen.

They were awakened at six in the morning by a noise coming through the ventilation grate of the executioner's team building temporary gallows in the central prison courtyard below them.

The absence of the morning reveille told everyone what was about to happen: someone was about to be killed. The question was: Who was about to be killed? Was it Bela, their brave leader?

Two inmates climbed onto the bunkbed and craned their heads toward the ventilation grate to listen. For thirty minutes, they could only hear muffled hammering and the occasional footfall. Then, silence.

Suddenly a voice, reading from the usual script, said: "The President of People's Republic has denied the request for a stay of execution!" Paul, Leslie, and Michael, who had all risked their lives to resist the communist takeover and were betrayed along with their leader, Bela, knew that there had been no request for clemency. Bela would not beg before the dictatorship's lackeys.

A clear and powerful voice rang out: "I die for my country! Jesus Christ, give me strength!" There was a loud crack of wood slapping against wood followed by silence.

The year was 1951, and the inmate, Paul, was my father.

Born in 1930 in Budapest, Hungary, my father was formed by the experience of war. When Hitler invaded Poland—a nation with centuries of ties to Hungary and many common noble families—my father hadn't even reached the age of ten. After the outbreak of hostilities, the government of Hungary maintained a formal neutrality. In practice, because Berlin had promised to restore to Hungary some of the territories taken from her after World War I, Budapest supported Germany and eventually declared war on both the Soviet Union and its Allies.

But by early 1944, the Regent of the kingdom of Hungary, Admiral Miklós Horthy, was no longer willing to be an accomplice to Hitler's Third Reich and the extermination of the Jews, and secretly approached the Allies to offer an armistice with his beleaguered nation. Sadly, the Hungarian initiative would never see the light of day as Hitler deployed his top commando, Otto Skorzeny, to Budapest to kidnap Horthy's son and force the regent to abdicate. The Nazis then occupied Hungary and installed a puppet government of fascists calling themselves the "Arrow Cross."

A country that had been the proud partner in the Austro-Hungarian Empire was now an occupied nation and a satrapy of the megalomaniac Austrian Corporal Adolf Hitler. Its once thriving Jewish community was corralled into ghettos before being murdered on the banks of the Danube or shipped in boxcars to the death camps.

This was the world of my father's childhood: a world of war and foreign occupation which shaped the man he became.

Both my parents died long ago, but I vividly recall my father's stories of the war years and my mother's account of the deprivation after the war; she was only six when it ended. These stories included escorting Jewish classmates who wore the Star of David on their jackets to school, protecting them from the abuse of German occupational forces. Others surrounded life after the siege of Budapest, when the invading Soviets had defeated the Nazis and took control of the country.

In 1945, my father, at the age of fifteen, was climbing through the ruins of the city with his best friend, Leslie, when a junior Soviet officer accosted them and pressed them into work. The boys were told to collect dead bodies and slide them into the basement of a bombed-out building that had been filled with lye and turned into a mass grave. When they had completed a full day of backbreaking work, the Russian officer took the boys to a field kitchen. On the way, they crossed paths with another Soviet officer who asked what was going on. When his colleague explained, the second officer began to shout and insist that the boys go back to the mass grave and work until it was full of cadavers. The two officers railed at each other until the first one pulled out his Tokarev service pistol and shot the second officer dead. He then led the boys to get their bowl of potato soup. This was a sudden and violent lesson in the value of life in Soviet culture.

By the time Hitler had been defeated, my father, having heard from his own parents about Hungary in the days of its freedom and having lived through the horrors of war on his doorstep, was praying for a rapid a return to normality. Especially after he heard of the Yalta Conference, at which the Allied leaders made a commitment that the countries of Central Europe would once again be independent and choose their own governments. But it was not to be.

In my first book, *Defeating Jihad: The Winnable War*, I chronicled my father's experience after the war—his arrest by the new communist regime, the torture, imprisonment, and eventual liberation by patriotic freedom fighters in the 1956 Revolution. Allow me to explain the effect his story had on me.

Most of my fellow Americans will find it hard to relate to the background that shaped my views. Unless, perhaps, you have served overseas in the armed forces in a region still plagued by dictatorship. Even so, less than one percent of our nation serves in the armed forces, and only a fraction of those are sent overseas.

It is hard to explain the lasting effect upon me of my father's answer to a question I asked as a young child when I noticed faint lines on his wrists. He responded, "That's where my interrogators hung me by the wrists, my hands tied together with wire behind my back from a pipe in the ceiling."

Or of walking into the rebuilt torture chamber in the basement of the erstwhile secret police headquarters in Budapest with my father, who had been brutalized there half a century earlier. I was a grown man and it was forty years since he had been tortured, but there we were in a reconstructed interrogation room where my father had been hung from pipes.

In spite of these traumatic experiences, the father I knew was always the fun one in any group. Growing up as an only child, I would watch from the top of the stairs as my parents hosted wonderful parties in our modest home in West London. My father regaled our guests so merrily that it was hard to believe he had lived through those years of horror in Nazi and then Soviet-occupied Hungary.

Susan, my mother and the daughter of a fellow political prisoner of my father's whose only crime had been being a leader of the Hungarian YMCA, was the consummate hostess. A truly incredible cook with a formidable intellect, she taught architecture, spoke seven languages, and relished art and fine culture. My father was a simpler soul, always ready with a risqué joke or a song and a subtle yet mischievous twinkle in his eye. And all this despite the death, destruction, and betrayal that he had witnessed, as the faint scars on his wrists attested.

I was only nine, the same age my father had been when World War II broke out, when the geopolitical significance of my father's life in Hungary was finally revealed to me. After four decades, I remember it so very clearly.

We were watching the evening news in our living room. My parents were very engaged with the world around them and my immersion in matters political started at an early age. It was November 1979, and the champion of Western democracy and all things British, Margaret Thatcher, was the prime minister. Just a few days earlier, a huge scandal had erupted when an investigative journalist revealed that the famed art historian and director of the Courtauld Institute, Sir Anthony Blunt, had been a member of the "Cambridge Apostles," a ring of Soviet spies during the Cold War which betrayed Great Britain and her allies. The scandal raged all the more forcefully because Blunt had admitted his guilt in 1964 in exchange for immunity from prosecution. The whole affair was kept secret from the British people for fifteen years.

The case of the Apostles, or "Cambridge Five," as they were called, was the most dastardly and damaging case of treason during the Cold War. The ring's members—Kim Philby, Donald Maclean, Guy Burgess, Blunt, and John Cairncross—had studied in Cambridge, where they were recruited to spy on the British government for the KGB. After graduating, four of the five joined the civil service, to include British intelligence, and betrayed the trust shown them by selling their nation to the Soviets.

When it was revealed that Sir Anthony, a fixture of high society, had been one of the spies and granted immunity, the prime minster was forced to respond publicly. In her statement to Parliament, Mrs. Thatcher confirmed Blunt's treachery, for which he would be stripped of his knighthood, but reassured the nation that his actions had never endangered any British lives.

As we watched the prime minister on television, my father said, "Oh, I know no British agents died. But hundreds of Hungarians,

Poles, Czechoslovaks, and Yugoslavs did." One of them was Bela Bajomi, hanged in the courtyard of the political prison in Budapest, as Leslie, Michael, and my father listened from their cell.

It was that statement by the head of the British government that spurred my father to write his own story, published in London as *Budapest Betrayed*. He detailed how as a teenager after the war, he saw the promises of Yalta—that occupied countries like Hungary would begin again in freedom—violated from the Baltics to the Balkans, as Nazi regimes were replaced by communist dictatorships.

THE COST OF RESISTING EVIL

Once the communists had fully taken over Hungary, my father started college. It was there he decided to resist the new dictatorship.

Identifying a handful of patriots among his fellow students, he helped Bela Bajomi organize a secret Christian resistance group. The plan was to covertly collect information on what the Communist Party was doing, how the Soviet troops were deployed across the country, and how the Kremlin was stealing the country's national assets and industries. The information would then be spirited out to a Western country, and when the world saw that Stalin was in breach of the treaties made at the close of the war, pressure could be applied against Moscow.

The members of the group succeeded in obtaining internships in strategic industries and offices crucial to the communist takeover. Bajomi managed to establish a secret line of communication to the United Kingdom. Soon enough, prosaic letters were being mailed at regular intervals to an MI-6 cut-out with the crucial data inserted between the anodyne script with an invisible ink. For several months, at great risk to their liberty and their lives, these young men, including my father, smuggled the truth out of captive Hungary with the hope that it would be used to weaken Moscow's grip and restore the nation's independence. But it wasn't to be.

As my father chronicled in his autobiography, the reports sent to London would eventually land on the desk of none other than Kim Philby: Soviet agent, Cambridge Apostle, and traitor to the West. Once he had received enough collateral information to identify the group's members by name, Philby betrayed them to his Soviet handlers, who then informed Moscow. When Moscow informed the Hungarian secret police, my father and his fellow patriots were arrested, tortured, and imprisoned. Bela, their leader, was executed.

At his trial, my father was also to be given a death sentence at the age of twenty. However, thanks to a well-connected great uncle, he was spared execution. Instead he received a "ten-year" sentence, which would have doomed him to die in prison since his classified sentencing document was stamped: "not to be released even after serving sentence." This document came into my father's hands after the communist regime fell in 1990.

As you can read in *Defeating Jihad*, my father spent two years in solitary confinement for being an "enemy of the state," following two years in a prison coal mine, and another two years in the main political prison outside Budapest. On October 23, 1956, the Hungarian people fought back against the dictators, and my father's and mother's lives changed forever.

After eight years of full-fledged communist dictatorship, several thousand students and factory workers banded together in an uprising that would become the Hungarian Revolution of 1956: the first attempt by a nation under Soviet occupation to free itself from the Kremlin. With captured weapons and homemade Molotov cocktails, the oppressed stood up to their oppressors, and for ten heady days, Hungary was free. The freedom fighters captured a Russian tank, battered down the prison gate, and liberated my father and his fellow prisoners of conscience from the hell of their communist confinement.

Hungary's freedom was short-lived, however. With hundreds of tanks called from Ukraine, Romania, and thousands of Soviet reinforcements, Moscow viciously crushed the revolution. Prime Minster

Imre Nagy and other leaders were kidnapped and murdered. Hearing that he too was on a shoot-to-kill list, my father escaped across the minefields into neutral Austria with his prison mate's seventeen-year-old daughter and future wife, Susan.

When asked in the refugee camp where they would like to live—unware that it was Philby in London who had betrayed them all—my father told the resettlement officer that they wanted to live in England. That is how I came to be born and raised in London, a British subject but Hungarian by family upbringing.

I didn't know the full story of my father's fight for a free Hungary or how he had suffered until the Blunt scandal erupted, prompting my father to write his book and share the shocking details of his childhood. But our home was often the location for reunions with onetime comrades and fellow prisoners like Father Bela Ispanki, the enigmatic Catholic priest and personal secretary to Cardinal Mindszenty, who was arrested and imprisoned for rallying Hungarian Christians against the communist dictatorship, and Laci, who had become a successful psychiatrist with a house on Lake Geneva. After the freedom fighters crashed through the prison gate with their Russian tank, Laci was made temporary prison warden whilst the true political prisoners were sifted from the common criminals, whom the revolutionaries were not keen on "liberating."

The values of my father and his compatriots formed the moral environment of my childhood. Tyranny, whether Nazi or communist, wasn't an abstract concept in a history book. It was the marks on my father's wrists. Resistance to dictatorship wasn't a vague platitude. I could touch it in the form of the tiny crucifix my father had carved out of a multicolored toothbrush handle in prison, Jesus' white body lying on the Bakelite blue of the cross. It was in the stories he shared of prisoners covertly collecting the raisins from their meals to make wine so the priests imprisoned with them, like Father Bela, could celebrate a secret Mass inside the prison. Determined to preserve our freedom, which he didn't take for granted, my father taught me how to handle a gun as soon as I could reliably hold one up and use it safely. He knew that all dictatorships want the population disarmed, and that a citizen without a means to protect himself and his liberty is not a truly free man. Thank you, Father.

And then there was my father's mode of interacting with the world. Despite the torture, the imprisonment, and the life of an exile, my father was amazingly "normal." He wasn't ever bitter or maladjusted. On the contrary, he loved the company of good people and perhaps trusted others a little too readily—more so than his cynical son, who had grown up in a free country. Despite all he had gone through, he told me that the only thing he was truly angry about was being deprived of the opportunity to row for Hungary in the Olympics. He had inherited his athletic ability from his father, Agoston, an Olympian and the fastest long-distance runner in Hungary between the wars. When my father was arrested at age twenty, he was a member of the Hungarian national rowing team. But I never saw him fulminate at what had been done to him. In fact, the only time I ever saw my father cry was when someone mentioned the name of Bela Bajomi, or of other fellow patriots who had made the ultimate sacrifice in the fight for freedom.

It was in this world that I learnt what justice is and that truth is not relative. From earliest childhood it was clear: evil walks the earth, and from time to time a man must resist it, often at great cost. That is why when the terror attacks of September 11, 2001, occurred, I processed them quite differently from my friends and those around me.

The perpetrators of the deadliest terrorist assault in modern times were connected in my mind to the totalitarians of the twentieth century, who had almost destroyed Judeo-Christian civilization. Yes, the al-Qaeda operatives did what they did in the name of a religion and not a godless ideology like fascism or communism, but the nineteen hijackers of 9/11 were brethren to the German soldiers who abused my father's Jewish friends. They were cut from the same cloth as the thugs who tortured him in the basement of the secret police head-quarters on Andrassy Street and partisans of a cause that would admit no compromise. Bin Laden's "soldiers," like Hitler's Gestapo, would kill or enslave you if you dared resist.

It was this perspective on the threat America and the West faced in the new century that would eventually bring me to the United States to explain that connection to the brave men and women of our military and law enforcement and what it would take to defeat the "new totalitarians." From the Green Berets of Fort Bragg to the Special Agents of the FBI, the analysts of the CIA, and the SEALs of the US Navy, I have shared the same message: "The loss of liberty is always but one generation away." There will always be those—whether they are Hitler's divisions, Stalin's spies, today's jihadists, or tomorrow's unknown threat—who would rob us of our freedom and destroy the values of our Judeo-Christian civilization if our vigilance flags.

IT WILL HAPPEN AGAIN AND WE MUST BE READY TO WIN

I was born in England, and Hungarian blood runs in my veins, but I am a proud American and legal immigrant to the greatest nation on God's earth. It was the highest honor of my life to serve as deputy assistant and strategist to President Donald Trump.

This book builds upon *Defeating Jihad,* but has a broader scope and a different structure. It is the product of my twenty-four years in the national security sector, both in government and in the private and academic sectors. It is a guide to the most important facts all Americans should know about the threats our nation faces now and will face in the future. But it is more than that.

Both the early nineteenth century Prussian General Carl von Clausewitz, in his classic work *On War,* and the ancient Chinese strategist Sun Tzu, in *The Art of War,* taught that the central aspect of all conflict is the will to win. To be sure, you must be able to inflict damage on your opponent—it is hard to defeat a tank with a bow and arrow—but the most important ingredient for victory is a will to win that is greater than your enemy's. From ancient Greece to the Vietnam War and to what we used to call the Global War on Terror, this has always been the case.

Yet having taught in our civilian and military institutions of higher education, such as Georgetown University and the National Defense University in Washington, I see America as a nation all too often forgetting this eternal truth. We fail to take seriously the key lines from the Marine Corps manual MCDP 1, *Warfighting*: "Although material factors are more easily quantified, the moral and mental forces exert a greater influence on the nature and outcome of war," which is "an extreme test of will."

To help correct that failure, I present here a handful of examples of men who had that crucial will to fight. Some are well known, such as Stephen Decatur, a central figure in a pivotal conflict early in the life of the nation, the Barbary Wars. Others are less famous but are of equal importance as exemplars: Chesty Puller, the most decorated marine in American history; Captain Eugene McDaniel, a naval pilot shot down in Vietnam who survived the horrors of Viet Cong prisons for six years; and Whittaker Chambers, not a warrior, but a hero nonetheless because of his resistance to totalitarianism and his commitment to the truth.

Their stories will provide inspiration for the new generation of defenders of the republic, a generation we all must encourage and build. For without an America of heroes ready to fight and win, the future will belong to those who serve the latest totalitarian incarnation of evil.

CHAPTER 1

Why We Must Always Be Ready to Fight

Si vis pacem para bellum.
If you desire peace prepare for war.

—PUBLIUS FLAVIUS VEGETIUS RENATUS

No right-minded person likes violence or the threat of violence. Nevertheless, there seems to be something about human society that predisposes us to use force again and again. On the individual level, violence is driven most often by avarice: the desire to obtain a material good without paying or working for it. At the collective level, when violence is used in a large-scale, organized fashion, the same motivation may hold: one community wishes to take the territory or wealth of another community. But there may be other reasons as well.

Human history is, in large part, the history of war. Over the millennia, the formation and development of human communities have been marked by wars between tribes, wars between city-states, wars between empires, and wars between modern nations. The last century can crudely be summarized as starting with World War I, in which the West lost a generation of young men in the trenches; proceeding through World War II, in which civilians were targeted on a massive scale and more than sixty million persons died; and concluding with four decades of the Cold War, a face-off between two alliance systems during which the horrific possibility of nuclear conflict haunted the whole world. At the fall of the Berlin Wall and the end of the Cold War, however, peace did not "break out." The end of the twentieth century saw hot wars of the intra-state variety break out in countries as far-flung as Yugoslavia and Rwanda, conflicts that killed more than a million human beings, often in the most barbaric of ways.

The opening of the twenty-first century offered little hope of a new, more peaceful age. On September 11, 2001, a handful of religiously motivated fanatics managed to execute the deadliest terrorist attack in world history. In less than two hours, almost three thousand people were killed in the synchronized attacks on New York and Washington. Since that infamous day that we now refer to simply as "9/11," America and her have initiated wars in Afghanistan and Iraq, deployed military units to numerous conflict zones in the Middle East and Africa, and initiated a military campaign against the jihadist insurgents of the Islamic State in Syria and Iraq. The first two decades of the new century seem to have marked a return to what specialists call "irregular war"— conflicts in which the enemy forces are not the conventional troops of another government, but terrorists and insurgents of non-state actors such as al-Qaeda or ISIS, the so-called Islamic State.

The purpose of this book is to help the reader understand the nature of war and America's experience with war since 1776, to spotlight former and current enemies, to identify what is necessary to defeat them, and to pay homage to those who have taken the fight to America's foes.

The master strategist Carl von Clausewitz famously described war as "the continuation of politics by other means." And yes, governments can pursue their national interests by war when all other options have failed. Yet war is much more than the calculated exercise of violence by nation-states. If years since 2001 have demonstrated anything, it is that war is not the preserve solely of countries and their governments. The violent enterprises of the Global Jihadist Movement (al-Qaeda, Boko Haram, and the Islamic State), cult-like terrorist groups such as the Lord's Resistance Army, and the pro-Kremlin "militias" fighting the Ukrainian army in Crimea can all be described as war.

Many people associate the word "war" with images from *Saving Private Ryan*: massed tank units engaging one another in the open and men in uniform fighting on a distant battlefield. They presume that armed conflict begins with declarations of war and ends with formal ceasefires and peace treaties. As we shall see, however, that type of war is historically the exception to the rule.

Over the centuries, most conflicts have been far less regularized than the world wars of the twentieth century or even the first Gulf War of the 1990s. Today's messy conflicts are more representative of mankind's past wars than the conventional and regularized conflicts we have spent so much time preparing our militaries to fight.

The untidy wars of the post-9/11 era do not fit well into the conventional understanding of why and how wars are fought and ended. Today there are no clear battle lines or fronts, enemy capitals to capture, or days to formally mark the end of hostilities and the return of our troops. Partially as a result of these changes and ambiguities, many question the rationale for our military engagements abroad and the new "national security" measures taken domestically in the name of our increased safety.

But it is indisputable that the world is a dangerous place and America will always have enemies. We need to understand them, deter them, and if that fails, vanquish them in battle.

WHAT IS WAR?

The *History of the Peloponnesian War* by the Athenian General Thucydides (c. 460–c. 395 B.C.) is still studied at military academies and war colleges around the world. In this remarkable chronicle of the war between Athens and Sparta, the great historian offers an explanation of why societies go to war. For Thucydides, there are three reasons to send men to kill other men. The first is *fear*—fear of what will happen if one does not fight. The second is *honor*—a concern to maintain or restore a society's prestige. The third is *self-interest*—the profit of the community. Any one or more of these motivations may be present in a given conflict. Thucydides' list seems reasonable to the layman, for these motivations appear to explain wars as diverse at World War II, the Vietnam War, and the post-9/11 Global War on Terror.

Adolf Hitler's invasion of Poland in 1939 can be explained as the pursuit of honor and self-interest, his desire to establish a "thousand-year Reich," and the need for more territory—*Lebensraum*—for his racially "pure" and inherently evil Aryan Empire.

In fighting the Vietnam War, America invoked the doctrine of "containment," which expressed our fear of the spread of communism (the "domino theory"), the global dominance of the Soviet Union, and possibly even a third world war.

US operations in Afghanistan after 9/11 were, at least initially, justified by the national interest,and even fear of, another mass-casualty attack on the territory of America, masterminded and organized in the al-Qaeda bases and training camps that the Taliban had allowed Osama bin Laden to build in their country.

If we move from antiquity to the modern age, we encounter another great general-author, the Prussian General Carl von Clausewitz (1780–1831). His posthumously published masterpiece *On War* is famous for the dictum cited above that war is simply "the continuation of politics by other means." This phrase, which has become a principle of modern war, is cited to explain violent conflict as just another function of the state: the option left to a government when other methods for achieving its objective have failed.

Clausewitz is also rightly famous for his observation that conflict is complicated by *friction*: the unforeseen challenges that make a war plan last only as long as first contact with the enemy, and by the *fog of war*: the lack of clarity and certitude on the battlefield which can be penetrated only by the skill of the military commander.

Perhaps the greatest sustained influence of Clausewitz's *On War* is an indirect one. The idea of war as "politics by other means" rests on the assumption that war is something governments decide to do, an assumption reinforced by what he called his "wondrous trinity." Adapting a construct that would be familiar to his Christian readers in Europe, Clausewitz described the nations that go to war as having three internal populations:

He assigns to each member of the trinity a fundamental characteristic:

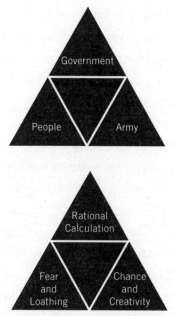

According to Clausewitz, a country's three key communities come together on the basis of their distinct traits in wartime.

The government, the political elite, makes the decision to go to war based on a reasoned calculation of the needs of the state (*raison d'état*). Politicians analyze the dangers and potential costs of going to war—or not going to war—and then make a rational decision.

The population is then mobilized to fight or support those fighting the enemy by fanning its hatred of the enemy.

Lastly, the professional military man, the commander, adroitly leverages and directs the hatred of the people to realize the reasoned interests of the state. He alone understands violent conflict and the role of chance, and he alone has the requisite expertise to manage the *friction* of the battlefield, to pierce the *fog of war*, and to lead his forces to victory.

Clausewitz's personal experiences shed light on his analysis of the mechanics of war. As a young man, he witnessed a new way of war. As a member of the most professional military organization of his day—the Prussian Army—he saw his beloved fighting force and its proud martial culture vanquished on the battlefield by the French forces under military genius Napoleon Bonaparte.

Bonaparte hadn't built an experienced and heavily institutionalized army to mirror the Prussian military establishment, but instead had introduced the practice of *levée en masse*, or mass conscription. Clausewitz witnessed Napoleon take ordinary civilians, total military amateurs, and rapidly turn them into a cohesive fighting force that beat the Prussian Army on the battlefield. The depth of this shock, in which the cream of European military culture had been violently displaced by a new way of war waged by conscripts, caused Clausewitz to focus on marshalling a people's unbridled passion to realize the rational political interests of the state. Hence, his conclusion is that war is the continuation of politics by others means. In other words, war is logical, organized violence.

But do politicians really wage war rationally? Has war always been the result of a cold and unemotional decision by political elite? There are those who differ with the Prussian general's understanding of war and do so quite strenuously and convincingly.

In a landmark work written more for the interested layman than the national security professional or the policy expert, the late British historian John Keegan laid down a comprehensive challenge to Clausewitz's consensus. Keegan, who wrote many works on the history of war and great military leaders, opens his famous book, *A History of Warfare,* defiantly: "War is not the continuation of policy by other means." He continues:

> [W]ar antedates the state, diplomacy and strategy by many millennia. Warfare is almost as old as man himself, and reaches into the most secret places of the human heart, places where self dissolves rational purpose, where pride reigns, where emotion is paramount, where instinct is king.

Today, experts and scholars are divided between those who consider Clausewitz's analysis enduringly valid—a camp most ably led by the British strategist Colin Gray—and those, best typified by the Israeli author Martin van Creveld, who see Clausewitz's relevance as limited to nation-against-nation conflicts, such as World War II, and having little to say about today's messier conflicts.

This argument will likely persist for some time. It is, however, instructive to assess what kinds of wars we have fought in recent centuries and what that experience can tell us about the wars America will have to fight in the future.

WAR: PAST AS PROLOGUE

In 1963, a professor at the University of Michigan took up the monumental task of collecting all the key data from all the conflicts and wars since the time of Napoleon. The resulting database, the Correlates of War Project now based at Penn State, is still being assembled today. This treasure trove of information is invaluable to anyone who wants to identify patterns and trends in war and peace over the last two centuries. And if you take the time to categorize the wars that the database contains, one remarkable fact stands out.

According to the project's definition, there have been more than 460 wars or armed conflicts since the end of the Napoleonic Wars in

1815. If you divide those conflicts into three groups—wars fought between countries, wars fought between countries and non-state groups or sub-state actors, and wars fought solely between non-state actors—you get a figure like this:

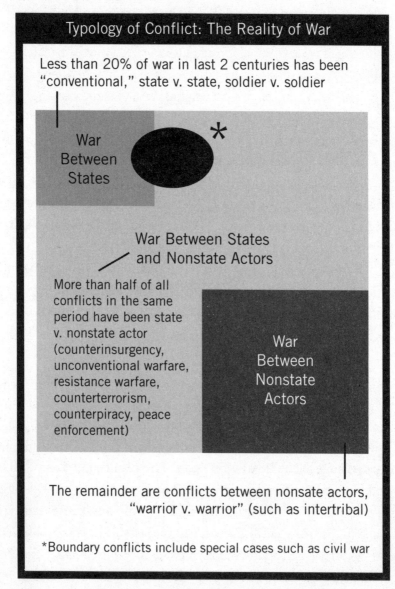

Types of War since 1815 (Based on data from the Correlates of War Project)

Specifically, of the 460 wars since Napoleon, less than twenty percent have been what we commonly understand as "conventional war," regularized conflicts between the uniformed armed forces of two or more opposing governments. More than 380 have involved the armed forces of a nation against an enemy that did not represent another country or government—a group like al-Qaeda, for example—or did not involve regular national armed forces at all, such as tribes fighting against each other. The empirical data therefore supports a critique of the Clausewitzian depiction of war as a rational enterprise carried on by the nation-state.

Keegan argues that war is rarely the result of reasoned calculation. Most often, war is fought for social and cultural reasons by non-state actors, often simply to assert one's identity in opposition to another group. To anyone who takes a look at the history of the Unites States from the longer perspective, the disproportionate ratio of non-traditional warfare to "regular" state-on-state war should not come as a surprise.

In the Pentagon's Hall of Heroes, the names of the more than three thousand Medal of Honor recipients are inscribed along the walls, each name listed under the campaign in which the honor was earned. Only five of the seventeen campaigns represented could be described as traditional state-on-state wars fought by regular armed forces fielded by their respective governments. These wars include World War I, World War II, and the Korean War. The other dozen conflicts are far from conventional, ranging as they do from our nation's involvement with the Boxer Rebellion in China to the Global War on Terror.

A more complete list of America's military conflicts—not just those in which the Medal of Honor was awarded—would look like this:

CONFLICT	Date
American Revolution	1775-1783
Barbary Campaigns	1801-1805 1815-1816
War of 1812	1812-1815

CONFLICT	Date
American Indian Wars	c.1817-1898
Mexican War	1846-1848
Civil War	1861-1865
Spanish-American War	1898-1902
Samoan Civil War	1898–1899
Boxer Rebellion	1900-1901
First Haitian Campaigns	1915-1934
Dominican Campaign	1916-1924
World War I	1917-1918
Nicaragua Campaign	1926-1933
World War II	1941-1945
Korean War	1950-1953
Vietnam War	1964-1975
El Salvador	1980-1982
Afghanistan Operation Cyclone	1979-1989
Desert Shield/Storm	1990-1991
Colombia	1990-1994
Balkans	1992-1994 (UN/NATO) 1995 (Deliberate Force)
Somalia Action	1993
Haiti Operation Uphold Democracy	1994–1995
Kosovo Campaign	1999
Operation Enduring Freedom	2001-2014
Operation Iraqi Freedom	2003-2011
Operation Inherent Resolve (Counter ISIS)	2014-

Even when the full list is categorized and we allow boundary conflicts as such as the Vietnam War to be counted in both the conventional and unconventional categories, it is obvious that irregular wars are in fact not irregular, but more common than the adjective would have you believe. The United States has fought in fifteen conventional and twelve unconventional conflicts—a fairly even split.

Additionally, it is worth remembering that one of America's earliest conflicts was the campaign against the pirates of the Barbary Coast, who bear a striking ideological resemblance to the Islamic jihadists of today's al-Qaeda and the Islamic State. The establishment of America as a free country was the result of a war in which irregular, often non-uniformed fighters waged a revolutionary campaign against the conventional, red-coated forces of the imperial government of Great Britain. In other words, the founding of the United States was the direct result of an eminently un-Clausewitzian war.

In light of the global data on war in the past two hundred years, and in particular, America's own history, it seems that we should reappraise the labels we use and rethink what kinds of wars we can expect to fight in the future.

The US military and the Pentagon use the term "conventional war" to describe conflicts like the First Gulf War or World War II, in which soldiers fight soldiers and tanks fight tanks. These are deemed to be "real" wars as opposed to "irregular" or "unconventional" wars, which are treated as anomalies to be handled by a small, elite group of fighters such as Army Special Forces (the "Green Berets") or their tri-service equivalents.

But why is this the case? Why do we officially call that which is more common "irregular" and that which is less common "unconventional"? Could this confusion explain some of our past military failures such as Vietnam?

It is clear that war in the past has more often resembled the wars we have been fighting since 9/11 more than the wars we fought in Europe during the twentieth century. In fact, most of mankind's armed conflict has been identity-driven violence waged by subnational parties rather than the uniformed forces of states.

So why do our institutions, and even our labels, favor "conventional" war? Simply because that is the kind of war we have been preparing to fight and that we prefer to fight. When decades and billions are spent preparing to do a certain thing, you will convince yourself institutionally that is what will be done.

Clausewitz was not an aberration. He was a product of an age in which city-states and empires were giving way to a new principle for organizing society: the modern nation-state. Evolving slowly out of the Peace of Westphalia of 1648, which closed several bloody decades of war between the Christian powers of Europe, the new international system would see loyalty and the locus of identity slowly shift from religion and feudal rulers to the nation of citizen and, eventually, to its representative government.

As the international political system progressed, the national elites of these new countries came to expect their future enemies to be other nations, other governments, and their regularized forces. Each country, therefore, built systems that would prepare it to fight the regular forces of another state should war become inevitable. In the West, the military culture began to de-emphasize war with irregular foes such as tribes or insurgent groups. We had regular armies and believed that we would be fighting regular armies in the future.

Over time, the Westphalian nation-state system brought about Westphalian security structures—means and methods for fighting other countries until every nation had an army, air force, and, if it was lucky, a navy. We allowed our internal military structure to shape our expectations of whom we would be fighting and how. The nations of the world, assuming that the new global system would continue to shape warfare, and ignoring the possibility that the kind of warfare that had predominated throughout history might again become the norm, developed military capabilities that are not suited to today's conflicts against al-Qaeda, ISIS, and other non-state actors motivated by ideology.

This book will explain how we need to adjust our fighting systems to deal with the resurgence of the older, more traditional types of conflict while maintaining our readiness for "conventional" war. At the same time, we will look at how information and technology have changed the practice of and public response to war.

Today a civilian, without a uniform, sitting in a control room in the American Midwest watching live footage from an unmanned aerial vehicle (UAV) flying over Afghanistan can decide in real-time to fire a missile from that drone at a target thousands of miles away. At the same time, if that missile should injure or kill innocent civilians, bystanders can instantly post photographs of the victims on the internet, igniting a furious and crippling public debate about the military campaign of which that UAV is just a small part.

This scenario is beyond the experience of the commanders and politicians of Clausewitz's age. How these new realities affect the way Americans think about, relate to, and ultimately support or oppose a military operation will be part of our discussion. At the same time, we will come to appreciate the lessons learned at great cost by Americans fighting for our country against unconventional foes and what it takes to win.

Stephen Decatur

To the Shores of Tripoli

Our war with jihadis did not start on that beautifully clear Tuesday morning of September 11, 2001.

Although it felt as though the events of that day in New York, Washington, Shanksville, and Pennsylvania marked a frightening new era and our entry into a new war, they did not. In fact, our country has been at war with religiously-motivated Muslim enemies for almost as long as it has been an independent nation.

Can you imagine Americans being held as slaves in foreign lands for years on end as our government, helpless to stop the kidnappings, paid tribute to the captors? This isn't some dystopian movie plot dreamt up by the febrile mind of a Hollywood scriptwriter. This is what happened to American seamen shortly after our birth as a free republic.

America's successful revolt against the British was historically remarkable. The idea that a handful of colonies could break the grip of the most powerful imperial force the world had ever seen must have seemed almost impossible to those who waged the Revolutionary War. But win we did.

That victory, however, was costly. The new country's treasury was depleted, and her ocean-going vessels, a crucial lifeline for the remote former colonies, no longer sailed under the Union Jack or enjoyed the protection of the Royal Navy. Almost overnight, American ships in the Mediterranean fell prey to the corsairs of the Barbary States, the Islamic principalities of North Africa, which had developed state-sponsored piracy into a high art. The Barbary pirates were afraid to disrupt the naval trade of the European powers, but they were happy to attack unescorted American vessels, steal their cargo, and make hostages or slaves of their crews and passengers. In fact, their audacity knew few limits.

In 1785, the year that America settled on the dollar as its new currency (the world's first decimalized currency), Mohammed, the Ottoman dey of Algiers, declared war on the United States, signaling that the Muslim-crewed corsairs patrolling the Mediterranean were free to attack American ships.

The Treaty of Paris had formally closed America's Revolutionary War only two years earlier, and the fledgling nation lacked the funds to build a long-range naval force able to protect its merchant vessels. Nor could it pay the tribute to the Barbary States that would guarantee safe passage of American ships. The pirates, therefore, proceeded to trawl the waters of the Mediterranean for defenseless American plunder. And they were successful for years.

But eventually, as she found her footing and Congress finally appropriated the requisite funds, our new nation began to build its navy: a navy that would take the war to the maritime jihadists with a force manned by young officers and enlisted men prepared to fight all the way to "the shores of Tripoli." One of the most gallant American fighters of this new warrior caste was Stephen Decatur.

Born in 1779 in Maryland to a naval officer of French descent and a mother of Irish lineage who had fled Philadelphia during the Revolutionary War, the young Decatur fell in love with the sea at the tender age of eight after accompanying his father on an Atlantic crossing. The die was cast, and eventually his passion for the sea and his love of country would carry Decatur to fame in our first war with a jihadi enemy.

After only a year of studies at the University of Pennsylvania, the young Decatur surrendered to his passions and became part of the team constructing the frigate *United States*, joining its crew as an eighteen-year-old midshipman on its commissioning in May 1797.

On the *United States* he learned the ways of the sea under the revolutionary hero Commodore John Barry, and a year later, almost to the day, Decatur was commissioned a lieutenant in the United States Navy by President John Adams. Within a few years, this navy numbered more than three dozen ships, and its commander in chief was Thomas Jefferson, who had had enough of the Muslim predations. Paying ransom and tribute to these petty potentates was, in his view, a shameful surrender to inferior adversaries.

In fact, Jefferson was well versed in the threat posed to America by the jihadists of North Africa. In 1786, when he was the US ambassador in Paris and the Barbary pirates were already attacking unprotected American vessels, he and John Adams, then our ambassador in London, asked the ambassador of Tripoli, Sidi Haji Abdrahaman, what right his co-religionists had to extort moneys from Western nations and to take Christians into slavery. They reported his reply to Secretary of State John Jay and Congress in a letter, reproduced in full as an appendix to this book, that has lain in unjustified obscurity, though every American ought to have reread it the day after the 9/11 attacks. Jefferson and Adams wrote:

> We took the liberty to make some inquiries concerning the Grounds of their pretentions to make war upon Nations who had done them no injury, and observed that we considered all mankind as our friends who had done us no wrong, nor had given us any provocation.
>
> The Ambassador answered us that it was founded on the Laws of their Prophet, that it was written in their Koran, that all nations who should not have acknowledged their authority were sinners, that it was their right and duty to make war upon them wherever they could be found, and to make slaves of all they could take as Prisoners, and that every Musselman who should be slain in battle was sure to go to Paradise.

This is the real reason Thomas Jefferson owned a Koran. No proto-multiculturalist, he simply wanted to understand the threat jihadism posed to his young nation.

More than a million Christians having been taken prisoner and enslaved by the North Africans, and finally in a position to do something about it, President Jefferson took action. On June 1, 1801, the first US naval squadron to cross the Atlantic—consisting of USS *Philadelphia*, *Essex*, *Enterprise*, and eventually *New York*—set sail under the command of Commodore Richard Dale, First Lieutenant Decatur assigned to the thirty-two-gun *Essex*. Their orders: to intercept and engage the Barbary pirates menacing American shipping. The First Barbary War was about to erupt.

Before the squadron reached North Africa, one of the Barbary States preemptively declared war on the United States. And with two warships already positioned off Gibraltar, Tripoli's forces were well-positioned to engage the US vessels. But when they were challenged by the American squadron, forced into the same harbor by adverse weather, the Tripolitan captains pleaded ignorance of the state of war. Given the speed of communications at that time, this could indeed have been true. But leaving the *Philadelphia* in the port to observe and guard the two Barbary warships, Dale and the rest of his squadron sailed on. The fate of the *Philadelphia* would turn Decatur into a national hero, a true American warrior who would sally into the heart of enemy territory and send the clearest of signals to anyone who believed that the new nation of America could be treated as a vassal and our people victimized.

OPERATION USS PHILADELPHIA: THE MARINE CORPS' FIRST COVERT ANTI-JIHADIST MISSION

In 1803, having run aground on a reef outside the port of Tripoli, the *Philadelphia* was captured by Ottoman corsairs and her crew taken prisoner. This time, America would not surrender. Decatur sailed for Tripoli with USS

Intrepid, disguised as a British merchant vessel, and USS *Syren*, carrying a handpicked team of marines. Mission: locate and liberate the *Philadelphia*. Or if that should prove impossible, destroy her so she could never be used against other US vessels or remain a prized trophy of the Tripolitans.

The *Intrepid*, piloted by a Sicilian who was included on the mission because he spoke Arabic, sailed into Tripoli harbor under a British flag as the sun set on February 16, 1804, its Marine Corps boarding party concealed below deck. The plan was to tell the Arabic-speaking harbormaster that the merchant vessel had lost its anchor and needed to shelter in the harbor to make repairs. Without raising suspicions, the disguised team drew closer and closer to the captured *Philadelphia* until they were miraculously allowed to tie their vessel to the Barbary booty of war. Darkness was all around; now was the time to strike and neutralize the corsair crew aboard the *Philadelphia*.

At just the right moment, Decatur yelled to his sixty marines, dressed as Maltese sailors, to board and recapture the *Philadelphia*. The Muslim pirates were taken totally by surprise, as the marines clambered aboard, swords drawn. The ship was recaptured in minutes, with only one American wounded and twenty Tripolitans killed.

As soon as the ship had been restored to its rightful owner, the United States Navy, Lieutenant Decatur realized that she could not be freed from where she lay; the *Intrepid* was simply too small to pull the *Philadelphia* out of the harbor to safety. But his instructions had been clear: if the *Philadelphia* could not rejoin the American fleet, no one would have her. And to that end, Decatur's special assault team had prepared a cargo of flammable materials with which to scuttle their sister ship.

Decatur gave the order: the incendiary packets were brought aboard the *Philadelphia* and strategically placed so as to ignite a rapid conflagration that would consume the ship before anyone from shore could save her. The bundles were set alight and the ship was abandoned. Decatur stayed aboard until the very last moment to ensure that no jihadi pirate would ever use her again.

Almost straightaway, the loaded cannon on the *Philadelphia* started to detonate in the massive fire that engulfed the ship. Cannonballs whizzed across the harbor and spread confusion among the Tripolitans as Decatur and his special mission team made their escape on the *Intrepid* and the *Syren*.

Mission accomplished. The *Philadelphia* would no longer be a part of the Barbary fleet or adorn the Muslim harbor. And the unprecedented audacity of Decatur and his team, doing all this right under the noses of the court of Tripoli—well, that would make any jihadi think twice about taking on the new might of the Unites States.

The young naval officer who, five thousand miles from home, led this special operations mission—one of our nation's first into Muslim territory—was barely twenty-five years old.

Vice Admiral, Viscount Nelson, the most celebrated British naval commander and hero of the Napoleonic Wars, is reported to have credited Decatur with "the most bold and daring act of the age." And Pope Pius VII, after so many Christians had been killed or enslaved by the Barbary states, observed that "the United States, though in their infancy, had done more to humble and humiliate the anti-Christian barbarians on the African coast in one night than all the European states had done for a long period of time."

As soon as Decatur arrived back on American soil, the secretary of the navy, Benjamin Stoddert, hurriedly recommended to President Jefferson that he be made a captain and the rank backdated to February 16, 1804, the night of the operation that restored America's honor after decades of humiliation at the hands of jihadis. Jefferson concurred, and with that the twenty-five-year-old became Captain Stephen Decatur, United States Navy, the youngest American ever to hold the rank.

Now you know just how long our brave sailors and marines have been at war with the forces of jihad and why the Marines' Hymn evokes "the shores of Tripoli," as our Devil Dogs were an integral element of the First Barbary War, not only in Tripoli, but the Battle of Derna and beyond.

CHAPTER 2

War Isn't Just about Guns and Bombs: When Ideas Kill

War is often motivated by more than dispassionate logic. Pride, fear, and hatred can mobilize an enemy far more effectively than a cold cost-benefit analysis.

Historically, most of the United States' foes have been driven not by rational motivations but by extreme ideologies. The Barbary pirates who terrorized American commercial shipping in the Mediterranean so soon after the Revolutionary War were just such a group. So were Adolf Hitler's Third Reich and Stalin's Soviet Union. Each regime was defined by an extreme, absolutist, and totalitarian ideology, as are Iran and North Korea today.

It is clear that a group like al-Qaeda, with its suicide bombers, or the Islamic State, with its goal of a global caliphate, is not a "rational" nation-state actor with conventional political interests corresponding to the Clausewitzian concept of war.

How do you deal with a foe who does not reason as you do? What is the role of force when facing an ideologically committed enemy, be it a unit of Nazi SS, the Viet Cong, or the 9/11 hijackers? Are there better options than all-out war against such an enemy? Perhaps there is no universal template for defeating such adversaries, but there are lessons to be learnt from America's past experience with totalitarian regimes and ideologically-motivated extremist groups.

If the threat from an enemy driven by a violent ideology is imminent and existential, there may be no alternative to large-scale conventional war. Nazi Germany posed such a threat.

WORLD WAR II: WAR FOR CIVILIZATIONAL SURVIVAL

The inability or unwillingness of European nations to challenge Hitler's rearming of Germany in the 1930s encouraged his territorial demands in the Sudetenland and the annexation of Austria. Once the Third Reich began its blitzkrieg across Europe, the response had to be one of tanks, infantry, bombers, fighter aircraft, and naval vessels. After Hitler's ally Imperial Japan attacked Pearl Harbor, this became a true "world" war as the United States eventually deployed more than twelve million fighting men to liberate Europe from the Nazis' ideology of Aryan racial supremacy and Asia from General Tojo's imperialism.

Although this global conflict would end only when the United States became the first nation to use nuclear weapons, World War II was not solely a war of tank divisions destroying tank divisions, of submarines hunting aircraft carriers, or fighter planes in aerial dogfights. A large part of the conflict involved the mind, not bullets or bombs. This was the propaganda war, and America became very good at "non-kinetic conflict."

WARS OF THE MIND

Clausewitz was correct that all war is a battle of wills. Propaganda has an important role to play in all conflicts since each side desires to influence the behavior and attitude of both its own people and those it wishes to defeat. The importance of propaganda grows when the enemy mobilizes its forces not simply to capture territory, increase its wealth, or avenge to a perceived injury, but in pursuit of an ideology that sees others as subhuman and for populations to be annihilated or subjugated, as was the case with Hitler's Nazi Reich.

Even in ostensibly conventional conflicts such as the first and second world wars, propaganda plays a crucial role. How successfully a nation contrasts itself and its military objectives to the enemy and the enemy's values strongly affects the duration and the human and economic costs of the war.

If carried out effectively, such non-kinetic "operations" can rouse a nation, undermine the forces of its adversary, and win over or deter the fence-sitters. The US Army's "I want you" recruiting poster, with its stern Uncle Sam pointing at the viewer, is among the most famous images in American history; more than four million were printed during World War I. Another is World War II's Rosie the Riveter urging American women on the home front with the slogan, "We Can Do It!"

Illustration 1: Perhaps the Most Famous Propaganda Poster

Illustration 2: Perhaps the Second-Most Famous Propaganda Poster

FROM PROPAGANDA TO MILITARY INFORMATION SUPPORT OPERATIONS

Today the word "propaganda"—Latin for "propagating"—has a pejorative connotation, suggesting communication that is tendentious and manipulative, but this was not its original sense. The word entered the English language in 1622 when Pope Gregory XV established the *Congregatio de Propaganda Fide*—the Congregation for Propagating the Faith—originally referring simply to activities that spread certain ideas amongst a given population. There was no suggestion of compulsion, deceit, or that the ideas were less than wholesome. The sinister sense that colors the word today is a product of the political history of the twentieth century, especially its association with two world wars and the totalitarian ideologies of fascism, Nazism, and communism.

Although arguments persist as to how "propaganda" should be defined, a simple and accurate interpretation would be: non-physical activities aimed at a specific audience with the intent of altering attitudes, behavior, or both.

To distance this important mission from the unpleasant and offensive propaganda of Hitler's fascist state and the former Soviet Union, today's national security establishment uses more modern labels for non-kinetic, information-based activities that support military objectives or broader national interests. These include:

- information operations
- strategic communications
- influence operations
- psychological operations

The last is often shortened to "PSYOP," or diluted into the dry-sounding Military Information Support Operations, or "MISO." The US Army Special Operations Command at Fort Bragg has at its disposal whole units whose mission is to use information in the battlefield directly against the enemy and win over local populations to the side of our forces or our allies' and partners' forces.

When attempting to strike the balance between military force and non-physical means to secure the country and realize national security objectives, it is useful to remember the grand strategist Sun Tzu's definition of the perfect victory: winning without fighting. How can this be done? How can you win without employing violence? By convincing your adversary—be it a country, terrorist group, or an insurgency—that it cannot defeat you or that its victory will be too costly.

You can also win the "battle of wills" if your adversary is convinced that its own values are bankrupt and yours are superior. This may sound impossible, but there is a twentieth-century example of a victory against a deadly foe won without ever firing a shot. This victory is of more than merely historical interest. Indeed, it is a case study of renewed importance for an age in which the general public is increasingly "gun-shy" of "adventurist" military operations abroad while the internet provides us and our enemies with a vast new arena for "influence operations."

WINNING WITHOUT FIGHTING: IDEOLOGICAL WARFARE AND THE COLD WAR

When the United States entered World War II, it joined the Soviet Union as an ally despite the Russians having signed a secret nonaggression pact with Hitler before the war which facilitated the carving up of Poland by the Third Reich and USSR. When Hitler betrayed the Kremlin and invaded the Soviet Union in 1941, Moscow became a de facto ally of the West. This alliance between the Soviets and America, however, would not endure.

The postwar takeover of national governments in Central Europe by communist parties under the Kremlin's control and Stalin's blockade of the American, British, and French sectors of occupied Berlin in 1948 clearly demonstrated the USSR's antipathy to America, its former ally. As the Soviets flouted the terms of the Yalta treaty, which was designed to bring peace and stability to postwar Europe, the spread of the Kremlin's influence and its ideology of communism became an urgent threat, first to the liberated nations of Western Europe, and eventually to the United States.

In the decades that followed, Europe was divided into a liberated West and East under dictatorial communist control. This bipolarity informed every dimension of geopolitics. Eventually a new balance of power emerged: the United States and her NATO allies on one side and the USSR and her vassal states of the Warsaw Pact on the other. This ideological confrontation provoked an enormous military buildup on both sides of the Iron Curtain. At the height of this arms race, America was devoting a tenth of its gross domestic product to defense, while the USSR committed at least a third of its national economy to its military.

At times, the standoff escalated frighteningly close to a kinetic war, even a nuclear exchange, as happened in 1962 when the Kremlin smuggled nuclear-armed missiles onto the island of Cuba, less than one hundred miles from the US mainland, undermining America's ability to respond effectively to a first-strike nuclear attack by the Kremlin.

There were also "hot" shooting wars during this Cold War, Korea and Vietnam being the most significant, with numerous others in Africa, the Middle East, and South Asia. These conflicts, however, were most often waged by proxies for the West and USSR. Remarkably, the main antagonists of this global standoff, America and the Soviet Union, never went to war directly with one other. At no time did the United States have to deploy forces in combat operations against the arrayed forces of the Kremlin or its client states in Europe. Yet, this conflict did eventually end with one side decidedly the victor and the other radically transformed—a happy outcome that was in large part the result of a successful and non-kinetic information campaign.

On one mild November evening in 1989, the Berlin Wall—which had for decades separated the citizens of the free world from those under totalitarian control—was peacefully breached. German families that had been forcibly divided when the communist government of East Germany erected the barrier to prevent its own citizens from escaping to the West came together that night to destroy the most infamous symbol of the Iron Curtain.

Why did the communist rulers of East Germany allow this? More importantly, why didn't the politburo in Moscow deploy tanks to crush those who demanded their freedom as it had done in Hungary in 1956 and Czechoslovakia in 1968? Why did the masters of the KGB and the gulags, who had been responsible for the deaths of millions of their own people, give up and allow their totalitarian system to fall? How did America and her allies win the war of ideas without firing a shot across Berlin's Checkpoint Charlie? How had we won the perfect victory, vanquishing our foe without resorting to violence?

The answer to all these questions is found in the realm of counter-ideological warfare. This non-physical approach to conflict is of great importance in the post-9/11 world. Ideology did not die on that November night almost thirty years ago. America faces old ideologically-driven foes, such as Iran and North Korea, as well as the new totalitarianism of global jihadism. And the USSR may have been transmuted into the much smaller Russian Federation, but the values and goals of its elite remain inimical to our republic.

HOW THE WEST WON THE COLD WAR WITHOUT FIRING A SHOT

The victory against the antidemocratic ideology of communism was a product of many years of resistance to the actions and influence of the USSR, including an arms race that drove the Soviet economy past its breaking point. But the key to the final victory was the Reagan administration's rejection of the longstanding US strategy of containing communism within its existing territory and decision to push back against Soviet power.

The USSR's invasion and occupation of Afghanistan in 1979 convinced the incoming administration that containment had utterly failed and that Moscow's power and influence could spread to other countries through military invasion or political subversion. Reagan therefore decided not only to assist the indigenous Afghan resistance in the largest CIA operation in history, but more importantly, to go on a global ideological counteroffensive to demonstrate once and for all the illegitimate nature of the regime in the Kremlin and the lies upon which its ideology of communism was built.

UNDERSTANDING THE IDEOLOGICAL THREAT AND WHAT IT TOOK TO WIN

After the Berlin blockade and communist takeover of the occupied nations of Central Europe clearly demonstrated that the Kremlin was no longer a friend to America, the new strategic response to Moscow was based upon an analysis of the USSR's ideological worldview by George Kennan, an American diplomat stationed in Moscow after the war. The State Department asked him to explain why

America's erstwhile ally was now acting like an enemy and seemed prepared to go to war over the control of occupied Berlin.

Kennan explained the Kremlin's "personality" in a classified telegram dispatched in 1946, known as the "Long Telegram." The following year, he published a modified version titled "The Sources of Soviet Conduct" in the influential journal *Foreign Affairs* under the pseudonym "Mr. X."

Kennan, who spoke Russian and had an intimate knowledge of the nation's history and culture, identified the ideology of communism as the greatest influence on the current and future behavior of the Kremlin, warning that it threatened Western democracies, including the United States. Because of its belief that communism and capitalism were inimical, the Kremlin was committed to systematically destroying or undermining democratic market systems around the world until communism was the only form of government left.

The USSR pursued global domination through a variety of means—direct military action, such as blockading the overland supply routes to Berlin, indirect military action, such as arming proxies and allies like North Korea and Cuba, and non-violent actions such as espionage, subversion, and propaganda to weaken America and her allies.

President Harry Truman relied on Kennan's masterly analysis in an address to a joint session of Congress on March 12, 1947, triggered by a growing communist threat to Greece and Turkey. In a speech that would shape American foreign policy and the national security stance of the Western world for decades to come, linking as it did the fate of the free world to American support for resistance to communism internationally, the president declared:

> The peoples of a number of countries of the world have recently had totalitarian regimes forced upon them against their will. The Government of the United States has made frequent protests against coercion and intimidation, in

violation of the Yalta Agreement, in Poland, Rumania, and Bulgaria.

At the present moment in world history nearly every nation must choose between alternative ways of life. The choice is too often not a free one.

One way of life is based upon the will of the majority, and is distinguished by free institutions, representative government, free elections, guarantees of individual liberty, freedom of speech and religion, and freedom from political oppression.

The second way of life is based upon the will of a minority forcibly imposed upon the majority. It relies upon terror and oppression, a controlled press and radio; fixed elections, and the suppression of personal freedoms.

Most importantly, Truman directly connected the fate of those threatened by communist takeover to the the safety of America:

We shall not realize our objectives, however, unless we are willing to help free people maintain their free institutions and national integrity against aggressive movements that seek to impose totalitarian regimes upon them. This is no more than a frank recognition that totalitarian regimes imposed on free peoples, by direct or indirect aggression, undermine the foundations of international peace and hence the security of the United States.

Finally the president concluded that US policy must support those prepared to fight against the spread of communism:

I believe that it must be the policy of the United States to support free peoples who are resisting attempted subjugation by armed minorities or by outside pressures.

The free peoples of the world look to us for support in maintaining their freedoms.

If we falter in our leadership, we may endanger the peace of the world—and we shall surely endanger the welfare of our own nation.[1]

This vision of assisting those who would resist the spread of communism around the world became known as the Truman Doctrine, and later as "containment policy." It led Truman and other US presidents, both Democrat and Republican, to support anti-communist movements and forces. Seeking to contain Soviet influence and the ideology of Marx and Lenin, American administrations often looked favorably upon—and at times facilitated—regimes that were less than democratic. Whether in Argentina or Iran, right-wing military regimes and other authoritarian governments were deemed as lesser evils compared with the globally ambitious dictators in the Kremlin.

In response to the the threat of communist expansionism, America helped form the North Atlantic Treaty Organization (NATO) and the Southeast Asia Treaty Organization (SEATO) to tie her allies and partners together in defensive relations that would strengthen their collective ability to protect themselves against Soviet attack. Containment, however, didn't help Afghanistan in 1979.

REAGAN'S PIVOTAL DECISION: FROM CONTAINMENT TO "ROLL BACK"

An unusual country comprising dozens of "nations" with dozens of indigenous languages, Afghanistan has been dubbed the "graveyard of empires," having over the centuries severely challenged the ambitions of imperial forces from Alexander the Great to the British Empire. Nevertheless, when the Kremlin deemed the socialist government in Kabul that had replaced the Afghan monarchy not "socialist enough," it decided to use its superpower military to make Afghanistan just one more of its enslaved satellite states.

After assassinating the Afghan president in December 1979, the Soviets sent eighty thousand troops, almost two thousand tanks, and as many armored personnel carriers to invade Afghanistan. It was now clear that America's containment policy had dramatically failed. The brand new Reagan administration decided that diplomacy and sanctions were not an adequate response to the emboldened and increasingly aggressive USSR. After authorizing a major covert operation, Reagan launched Operation Cyclone. This operation was co-funded by the kingdom of Saudi Arabia, run with the Pakistani intelligence service, and used weapons purchased from China and Europe to provide sustained support to the indigenous Afghan fighters in their resistance to their Soviet occupiers.

In addition to arming and directly supporting the fight against communism's spread into the region, the Reagan administration increased defense spending in general. The goal was not simply to achieve military superiority over the USSR, but also to place an increasing financial and economic stress on the creaking command economy of the Marxist state. The new investment in America's defenses went to personnel and established weapons systems and new technologies that would challenge Moscow's capability to compete, let alone catch up, with America militarily.

The most famous of these new technologies was the Strategic Defense Initiative (SDI), the missile-defense system that Reagan's critics derisively labelled "Star Wars." SDI was an effort to assemble a system that could intercept and destroy Soviet nuclear-armed missiles in flight, obviating any Soviet plan for a preemptive strike against America and the West.

Its detractors ridiculed the system as a pipe dream, but the politburo in Moscow took it very seriously indeed. General Secretary Mikhail Gorbachov abruptly ended his nuclear arms negotiations with President Reagan at Reykjavik in 1986 rather than accede to further US research on SDI. That research would later spur significant advances in sensor technology, lasers, and such cutting-edge weapons as the future "railgun" platform.

WINNING WITHOUT FIGHTING

Perhaps the least appreciated of the Reagan era responses to the increased aggression of the Soviet Union are the non-physical ones. In 1977, former Governor Reagan, preparing for another run at the White House in 1980, remarked to Richard Allen, his future national security advisor, "My theory of the Cold War is we win and they lose." Reagan was not thinking of winning a "hot" war with the USSR, but an ideological war. It would be necessary for the United States to deploy non-kinetic means to demonstrate the moral and economic bankruptcy of the Soviet regime.

After the giant covert mission in Afghanistan, increased defense spending, and the development of defensive technologies that made Russian strategic advances irrelevant, the Reagan administration turned aggressively to the "war of ideas." What we did then as a nation is of great relevance today as we face post-Cold War adversaries who know they cannot defeat us militarily but are conducting information operations and trying to subvert us in unconventional ways.

As George Kennan's Long Telegram and the Truman Doctrine recognized, the enemy's ideology was fundamentally illegitimate. Under the communist system, the wishes of the people did not matter. Only one party could exist, and the Communist Party elite held the monopoly on power and "truth." Any dissension with the party would lead to persecution, labor camps, or execution. Yet at the same time, the Soviet Union and her frontmen and agents in other "captive nations" continually preached equality, peace, and justice. Reagan understood that the gulf between communism's depiction of reality and the plain truth was the enemy's greatest vulnerability. The Kremlin preached equality for all in a classless society, yet there was obviously a tiny elite for whom all luxuries were available whilst the majority stood in line for hours to buy the staples of life. Shining a light on that disparity would illuminate the bankruptcy of the Soviet "narrative."

At international conferences and diplomatic engagements, sundry high officials of the Soviet bloc spoke endlessly of human rights and peaceful coexistence. Meanwhile, their citizens were tortured and imprisoned for their beliefs, and Soviet "allies" such as Hungary, Czechoslovakia, and most recently Afghanistan, were invaded because they did not obey the diktats of the Kremlin. Just nine years after Reagan assumed the presidency, a strategic American counteroffensive targeting these contradictions would help bring the whole dictatorship down without bombers or tank divisions.

This non-physical counteroffensive worked at various levels. At the highest were the top-secret presidential directives that outlined the plan to discredit the Kremlin, demonstrate the injustice of the communist regimes, and reinforce the nascent pro-democracy forces behind the Iron Curtain, especially the Solidarity trade union movement in Poland. These covert measures were complemented by the president's speeches undermining the prestige and power of the communist elite, most famously his "evil empire" address and his dramatic entreaty in front of the Brandenburg Gate in Berlin: "Mr. Gorbachev, tear down this wall!"

This two-pronged assault—open denunciations of communist tyranny and behind-the-scenes operations to weaken the stranglehold of the Kremlin—was reinforced by increased counter-propaganda broadcasts by the congressionally-funded Radio Free Europe (for Central and Eastern Europe,) and Radio Liberty (for the Soviet Union itself). These broadcasts in the languages of the captive nations often featured former dissidents who had escaped the "workers' paradise" and could speak firsthand of the internal contradictions and illegitimacy of the socialist state.

In addition to these measures, the Reagan administration authorized a systematic attack on the propaganda that the Kremlin had been spreading for decades. The vehicle for this assault was a small interagency organization which today has new relevance in the fight to delegitimize the totalitarians and ideologues who threaten us.

HOW TO KILL BAD IDEAS: SMALL IS BEAUTIFUL

The US approach to delegitimizing the anti-democratic message of our Cold War foe was logical and comprehensive. As the "front-man" for America, President Reagan made the strategic-level argument about the Soviets' moral bankruptcy, a role for which the former actor now remembered as the "Great Communicator," was perfectly suited.

For example, when he demanded that his Soviet counterpart tear down the wall that separated East from West in Berlin, his global audience on both sides of the divide knew full well that he wasn't delivering a throwaway line. Calling attention to the Berlin Wall so dramatically underscored the harsh geopolitical reality that the communist elite had built a wall not to protect its people from the predations of a capitalist West, but to prevent their escape from a totalitarian regime to the free world.

At the same time, it was understood on the basis of Kennan's analysis that in a one-party state such as the USSR or any of its Warsaw Pact satellites, the party could brook no dissent and therefore had to monopolize all information. In a system without freedom of choice, a free market, or independent media, all information was controlled by the state. All domestic media were party-sanctioned and controlled. Foreign media were banned, and anyone found listening to them or reading them would be punished.

Several of the nations now under communist control had once been democracies or at least moderately open societies, and Washington expected that their populations would crave uncensored news from the outside world. The Reagan administration therefore redoubled America's commitment to broadcasting behind the Iron Curtain, investing in new pro-democracy channels such as Radio Martí, broadcasting in Spanish into Cuba and modernizing Radio Free Europe, Radio Liberty, and the English-language Voice of America.

In the Reagan era, America's ideological orchestra had a highly visible conductor, and the strains of the symphony of freedom floated across the airwaves throughout the Soviet empire, finding an eager audience.

Having recognized the failure of containment and replacing it with a policy of "rolling back" Moscow's influence globally, the White House identified Soviet propaganda as a direct threat to free nations everywhere and in 1981, established the Active Measures Working Group (AMWG) to uncover and undermine these global influence operations.

In Soviet terminology, "active measures" included any political actions aimed at influencing foreign populations or foreign political elites in the interests of the Kremlin and the spread of communism into new territories. By the 1980s, active measures included not only the firsthand propaganda efforts of Soviet government organs such as the KGB and the diplomatic corps of the USSR, but also:

- the use of front organizations representing themselves as apolitical
- co-opting agents in the West and the non-aligned third world, especially in media and academia
- the aggressive distribution of forged documents to support stories undermining America and her allies

Key figures in the Reagan administration realized that the general public in the West and third-world nations had little idea how aggressively the Soviets were manipulating public opinion through their surrogates and covert assets. The AMWG was a small and truly interagency group, made up of representatives from the Department of State, Department of Defense, CIA, FBI, US Information Agency (USIA), Defense Intelligence Agency, and National Security Council.

Meeting every week and working hand in hand with expert staffers from Congress, the AMWG developed the "RAP" system—report, analyze, publicize—to win the war of ideas. American Information Centers, operated by the USIA in cities around the world, submitted reports on local Soviet and Warsaw Pact disinformation efforts to Washington's Bureau of Intelligence and Research (INR). INR experts, assisted by the CIA and Soviet defectors, analyzed these reports, identifying lies, fabrications, and inconsistencies. The AMWG then publicized these findings, exposing the communists' stories as disinformation that could be sourced right back to Moscow.

The AMWG shed light on a wide array of past and present Soviet influence operations. These included Moscow's use of the putatively independent and apolitical World Peace Council to block the deployment in Europe of intermediate-range nuclear forces, which were a key deterrent of the USSR and subordinate Warsaw Pact militaries.

The list of forgeries and lies identified and exposed by the RAP process bears some scrutiny, as it includes the kinds of stories that even today, like reanimated zombies, live on in the internet world of insidious conspiracy theories.

The reports of the AMWG proved, for example, that the Soviets had spread stories that the CIA was responsible for the Jonestown cult's mass-suicide in Guyana in 1978 and that the US government was smuggling in Latin American children just to butcher them and harvest their organs for transplants.

Perhaps the most famous influence operation uncovered was a story, fabricated in Moscow and seeded among the press in Africa, that the AIDS virus was a product of US biological weapons experimentation. By forensically tracing the story to its Soviet source and demonstrating the forgeries and outright lies on which it was constructed, the AMWG delivered a direct blow to the Soviets' credibility and moral prestige. The implication was clear: if "Moscow Central" could systematically lie about something as tragic as the international AIDS epidemic, how seriously should anyone take its public statements and commitment to causes such as world peace or social justice and equality? A regime that was prepared to exploit AIDS or the Jonestown tragedy was clearly immoral and not to be trusted.

VICTORY IN THE SUN TZU WAY

On November 9, 1989, the strategy of undermining the communist ideology while applying the pressure of SDI and an American arms build-up finally bore fruit.

That night, on the very spot where Ronald Reagan had called out Mikhail Gorbachev, striking a death blow to the legitimacy of the Soviet regime, the Cold War ended. And it ended without one shot being fired from the barrel of an American M-16 or a Soviet AK-47. Not one missile was launched, not one combat plane scrambled. The residents of Berlin, not waiting for Mr. Gorbachev's help, began to tear down that wall. Communist border guards, who before that night would have shot anyone attempting to escape to the West, simply stood by and watched, their masters having lost the will to order them to use force. Thus had our enemy lost the will to fight, to die for the bankrupt vision peddled by its decrepit and morally vanquished elite. A totalitarian ideology had been brought to its knees without the need to resort to war.

Today, facing ideological foes once more, we have much to learn from this mode of war. As our new commander in chief develops his own Trump Doctrine, his team would be wise to learn from President Reagan's example and from the techniques developed under the Active Measures Working Group.

Chesty Puller

*The Marine Legend Who Turned
the Tide in the Pacific*

Some men are born warriors.

The male is the more aggressive sex, but few men are sculpted in granite with a spine of steel.

It is said that bravery is not the absence of fear, but the capacity to act despite one's fear. That may be true. But there are those who naturally embrace danger, who instinctually run toward the gunfire. Lewis "Chesty" Puller epitomizes that type of man as the most decorated marine in the history of the United States Marine Corps and the only American awarded the US Army Distinguished Service Cross and the Navy Cross five times.

Born in West Point, Virginia, Lewis Puller tried, and
failed, to join the army at age sixteen during the Border
War with Mexico. His mother prevented this attempt by
withholding her consent for the young man to enlist. So
instead, he enrolled at the Virginia Military Institute in
1917, enlisting in the marines the next year with the hope
of going "where the guns are!" The First World War
ended, however, before the stocky and barrel-chested
"Chesty" could be deployed.

But Corporal Puller would indeed see duty overseas,
as he was shipped out to Haiti to train with and fight
alongside the local paramilitary gendarme forces in dozens of skirmishes. After proving his mettle as an NCO,
he began his career as a Marine Corps officer when he
was recalled stateside to be commissioned a second lieutenant.[1]

But foreign ports beckoned once more, and the young
officer left for the first of multiple tours in Nicaragua to
fight alongside the local national guard in the unconventional war with Augusto César Sandino's guerrilla forces.
It was here that "Chesty" would earn his first Navy
Cross for leading his marines in no fewer than five battles in which he and his men were greatly outnumbered.
"[T]he bandits were in each engagement completely
routed," read the citation that accompanied his medal.

He earned his second cross in the last major battle
with the rebels, near El Sauce. The citation recounts the
young marine's intrepidity in unusual detail:

> Lieutenant Puller and his command of forty
> Guardia and Gunnery Sergeant William A. Lee,
> United States Marine Corps, serving as a First
> Lieutenant in the Guardia, penetrated the

isolated mountainous bandit territory for a distance of from eighty to one hundred miles north of Jinotega, his nearest base.

This patrol was ambushed on 26 September 1932, at a point northeast of Mount Kilambe by an insurgent force of one hundred fifty in a well-prepared position armed with not less than seven automatic weapons and various classes of small arms and well-supplied with ammunition.

Early in the combat, Gunnery Sergeant Lee, the Second in Command, was seriously wounded and reported as dead.

The Guardia immediately behind Lieutenant Puller in the point was killed by the first burst of fire, Lieutenant Puller, with great courage, coolness and display of military judgment, so directed the fire and movement of his men that the enemy were driven first from the high ground on the right of his position, and then by a flanking movement forced from the high ground to the left and finally were scattered in confusion with a loss of ten killed and many wounded by the persistent and well-directed attack of the patrol. The numerous casualties suffered by the enemy and the Guardia losses of two killed and four wounded are indicative of the severity of the enemy resistance.

This signal victory in jungle country, with no lines of communication and a hundred miles from any supporting force, was largely due to the indomitable courage and persistence of the patrol commander [Lieutenant Puller].

Such a remarkable record of bravery would satisfy most marines, but not the man who would become the legendary General Chesty Puller.

The young Devil Dog's early career was typically heterogeneous, with stints at Fort Benning, Georgia; the facility later known as Camp Lejeune, North Carolina; Quantico, the crossroads of the corps; aboard USS *Augusta*; and even in China, commanding a marine detachment in Beijing and later in Shanghai.

Puller's experiences and acumen led to promotions and command of the First Battalion, Seventh Marines, (the "1/7") of the First Marine Division, by which time the United States had entered the Second World War.

The year after the attack on Pearl Harbor, where he had served before the war, Chesty's actions led to the rescue of three companies surrounded by Japanese forces along the Matanikau River on Guadalcanal. He called in fire from offshore vessels, which allowed smaller craft to approach the shore for an amphibious evacuation of the units trapped behind enemy lines. This action earned him a Bronze Star. But yet to come was his greatest feat, an act of bravery against seemingly insurmountable odds, for which a third Navy Star was pinned to that formidable chest. More importantly, the outcome of that battle turned the tide of the war in the Pacific in the favor of America.

At this point, it is important to remember whom we were fighting in the Pacific. When we think of World War II, we usually think about the European theater. Its hold on our imagination is no doubt the result of the horrifying evil of the Nazi regime and the spectacular allied invasion on D-Day—the largest combined arms invasion in human history—which launched the final drive to victory.

But the Pacific theater and our imperial Asian enemy were as much a part of America's war experience as the battlefields of Europe. And, of course, the blow that brought the hostilities there to an end—the atomic bombing of Hiroshima and Nagasaki—marked the beginning of a new epoch.

The Pacific theater and our Asian foe were horrific. The inhumanity of Tojo's forces—thousands of prisoners of war brutalized in the Bataan Death March, human experimentation and biological weapons research on live subjects by military Unit 731, thousands of civilians and POWs worked and starved to death on the Burma Railway, the torture of prisoners and the wanton execution of captured airmen in contravention of the Hague Convention and the laws of war—was exceeded only by the executor's of Hitler's "Final Solution."

This was the savage foe that the now Lieutenant Colonel Puller faced down during the strategically pivotal battle for Henderson Field.

By the end of October 1942, the situation on Guadalcanal had swung back and forth repeatedly, with the situation no longer looking good for US forces. In early August they had taken Henderson Field, a critically important airfield now protected by Puller's men, a sole battalion of the First Marine Division. But the Japanese wanted it, and they had the forces to take it. The order was given to the Imperial Sendai Division to destroy the Americans and take and hold the airfield.

Short on food and water, menaced by malaria, and exhausted from building defensive redoubts around the airfield, the 1/7 was stretched thin by the night of October 24. Dozens of men had already been lost in ninety minutes of long-range shelling from the fourteen-inch guns of the

Japanese battleships *Haruna* and *Kongo* and Japanese aerial bombardments. The 1/7, moreover, had no organic reserve element in case it was overrun. But Colonel Puller was most definitely in charge.

The commander, with the steely gaze and a crooked smile that sneaked through now and again, maintained morale. He made sure his men kept themselves clean-shaven and presentable, proud of their composed and steely response to Tojo's onslaught. He also ensured that worship services were available to those leathernecks who wished to call on reinforcements of a higher order in a war that truly was between the forces of good and evil.

But still, the odds were not in the 1/7's favor. Japanese vessels managed to drop ammunition and supplies for the forces preparing to attack Henderson Field, and the so-called "Tokyo Express" ferried thousands of reinforcements with which to retake the airstrip. Now the Sendai Division could count on the support and diversionary maneuvers of three infantry battalions moving up from an inland strong-hold. Two more battalions and a Japanese tank company swept in along and across the mouth of the Matanikau River, encircling Puller and his remaining men, as the divisional assets swept up what they thought was an undefended southern flank.

And on the afternoon of the twenty-fourth, as a monsoon-like rain began to fall, thousands of Japanese soldiers, who had been told by the Sendai Division's commander, Lieutenant General Masao Maruyama, to win or not come home, marched on the marines. The battle for Henderson Field had been joined.

With human assets far outnumbering the brave marines under Puller's command, the Japanese employed the human wave approach. By three o'clock a.m., they had executed half a dozen major assaults on the encircled 1/7. In the days before the attack, Puller's men had emplaced machine guns, sometimes resurrecting broken weapons and scavenging others from aircraft downed on the island. These produced formidable arcs of fire, reinforced by artillery and mortars. But now, ammunition was dangerously low and many of the guns were wearing out or overheating. If victory could not be won rapidly, there was nowhere to retreat to, and the colonel knew it. Although the Third Battalion of the Army's 164th Infantry Regiment had been rerouted to support Puller and his men, there was no "plan B." If the 1/7 and their cousins from "Big Green" couldn't hold off the emperor's forces, the airfield would be Japan's and Guadalcanal would most likely be lost.

The battle lasted for another two days. Wave after wave of Japanese assaulters forced Puller to reposition his forces, send out new scouts, and relieve those who were on the verge of collapse. But it worked. The marines fought through the onslaught, the barrages, and the repeated frontal assaults, led by a man who refused to countenance defeat and surrender the airfield to General Maruyama.

At the end of it all, more than 2,500 Japanese soldiers had been killed. Puller had lost twenty-four marines killed in action, with two missing and twenty-eight wounded—an incredible ratio of destruction that marines have admired ever since.[2]

Surprisingly, one Japanese officer thought the Americans lacked initiative, but admitted "they do more duty than they are told."[3]

Chesty Puller was awarded his fourth Navy Cross after the battle of Cape Gloucester and then went on to command the First Marine Regiment, the Infantry Training Regiment at Camp Lejeune, and the marine presence at

Pearl Harbor. But his battles were far from over. He served courageously yet again during the Korean War, receiving the Silver Star for his leadership during the landing at Inchon. The US Army awarded him the Distinguished Service Cross for heroism, and he received a fifth Navy Cross for his actions during the battle of Chosin Reservoir in 1950. The following year, he was made brigadier general and came home to take command of the Third Marine Division at Camp Pendleton. Two years later, he was promoted to major general, and by 1954, he was in charge of the Second Marine Division at Camp Lejeune. The next year, a stroke forced his retirement from his beloved corps after almost four decades wearing its uniform.

Chesty Puller died in 1971, receiving his third and final star posthumously. From private to lieutenant general, the most decorated marine in history, a leader of men, a living legend. An American.

Chesty isn't an inspiration solely at the individual level of American hero. His actions and unswerving commitment to our nation must be placed in its proper context, especially the significance of his role in winning the battle for Henderson Field.

Chesty understood what would happen if Hitler's Germany and Hirohito's Japan won: the darkness of dictatorship would descend over the free world. The eternal values upon which our republic was founded would be snuffed out like a solitary candle.

America may have joined the war late, but without its marines and GIs and unstoppable economic engine, the Axis would have won the second War for the World. And in the Pacific War, Guadalcanal was the foothold that could not be lost, and Henderson airfield was the jewel that could never be surrendered.

The victory by Puller and his marines in October 1942 presaged the defeat of Japan. This was the battle that ensured that America would not only keep the ground it had recaptured from its enemy, but win and maintain naval and air superiority over the Solomon Islands and then the Southern Pacific. Without that, our "island hopping" campaign would have been impossible. And without the success of that campaign, hundreds of thousands of marines and GIs would likely have died and the war would have lasted even longer than it did.

General Tojo and Admiral Yamamoto wanted Henderson Field, but Puller and his marines held it. The Japanese failure there marked the end of their commitment to Guadalcanal. That implicit surrender signaled their lack of capacity and overall will to win.

One man, part of the Marine Corps family, leading our nation's marines, turned the war and made victory over evil a reality. That is who we are.

CHAPTER 3

What Do You Need to Know about War?

The events of September 11, 2001, the rise of groups like ISIS, and the growing belligerence of nation-state actors such as Russia, Iran, and China have Americans searching for a measure of geopolitical certainty in an increasingly unpredictable and "unconventional" world. We look back longingly to an age in which the battlefield was understandable, in which we thought we knew the enemy, the methods and means at his disposal. Even now, almost a generation after 9/11, fundamental questions remain unanswered. What is the nature of our enemy—or enemies? What are the long-term objectives of those who wish us ill? Are the threats America faces mostly to be found abroad or here at home? Do we have the right tools to keep our nation's treasure and loved ones safe?

FIRST, LOOK IN THE MIRROR

If we turn once more to Sun Tzu to answer such fundamental questions, we will find that we must start with ourselves. We must understand who we are and what we represent before we can identify what threatens us and our value system. The gross if superficial outline is clear. Today, America is the world's sole superpower. Yet despite its immense power advantage over other states, on 9/11 it suffered the deadliest "irregular" attack in modern history. Almost two decades later, it is still involved in two nontraditional conflicts, one in the Middle East and one in Central Asia. Neither of these regions dominated the work of military planners during the decades of the Cold War. At the same time, America is focusing much of its remaining national security capacity on neutralizing the threat of terrorist attack against the homeland.

But who we are and, therefore, where we need to seem to be difficult questions to answer, especially for those in Washington who are meant to know. Yet we must understand our own context beyond the most topical "crisis of the day" and at a level of analysis deeper than that supplied by the mass media or sundry talking heads.

This exercise in national self-understanding necessarily concerns the "strategic culture" of the United States. After all, strategic culture influences how we approach threats, and it challenges and shapes our responses. But after the events of the past seventy years, it is just as important to understand the evolution of US strategic culture, which has been far from static since 9/11.

World War II and the Cold War left our country emphasizing firepower, technology, and nuclear deterrence—a posture that was distinctly unsuited to the very different strategic reality that emerged in the 1990s. Now, we must honestly assess how the intelligence-gathering and forecasting habits of World War II and the Cold War have impeded our warfighters in the missions they are expected to execute today. We have invented new capabilities, such as offensive unmanned aircraft systems and stealth technology, and we have written new doctrine for current missions, but we have not yet fundamentally reworked the architecture and culture of a national security establishment designed primarily to defeat the armies of other countries.

THE BROADER CONTEXT

In addition to delving into the premises of our strategic culture, we must examine the context in which the rest of the world finds itself at the beginning of the third millennium. Without wandering into the black art of long-range projection, we must ask the right questions about relative power, the role of ideology, and the influence of demographics on actors who in the past were not of concern to us or, in that age of bipolar conventional military standoff, simply did not exist. Nation-state actors and non-nation state actors alike are affected by geopolitical changes. Power can no longer be measured simply in terms of gross domestic product or numbers of tank regiments.

Lastly, and perhaps most difficult of all, it is the duty of all senior officials involved in providing for national security to seriously and candidly reassess the assumptions upon which our existing systems of analysis and planning are based. We must evaluate how apt these central concepts still are and formulate new principles should they be found wanting. And this is a task not only for the elite. If we are to be responsible citizens and voters, we too much understand how the world has changed since the Cold War.

We must recognize that no concepts beyond the core values enshrined in the Declaration of Independence and the Constitution are immune to critique and reappraisal when it comes to securing the homeland. America's founding values are sacrosanct and immutable, yet we must be ever imaginative and flexible in how we realize and protect them. For example, if the "wondrous trinity" of Clausewitz is not relevant for an age of globally dispersed non-state actors like al-Qaeda or ISIS and cyberwarriors such as the worldwide hacker group, Anonymous—the likes of which the Prussian theorist could never have imagined—it must be discarded or at least substantially reworked.

A survey of our current context should also include century-long trends. The blogosphere, professional military education journals, and civilian publications provide ample reading on how irregular warfare differs from conventional warfare. Nevertheless, we must move beyond the theoretical navel-gazing of purely semantic debates. When Clausewitz delivered his immortal dictum that war is "the continuation of politics by other means," he was writing in a specific historical and socioeconomic context. No matter how useful his analysis may seem, it cannot be divorced from the age in which it was born—an age when conventional war dominated strategic thought.

Clausewitz's *On War* must be understood as one man's forceful attempt to impose meaning on the clash of national arms. More specifically, it must be appreciated as the intellectual pilgrimage of an officer seeking to explain the destruction of his professional military culture by an upstart foe using the radical approach of *levée en masse*. That is exactly why Clausewitz sees rational governmental ends behind the actions of his skillful commander, who harnesses the passion and hatred of his troops (the population).

Since the Westphalian concept of the nation-state informs everything Clausewitz wishes to achieve, we are justified in reassessing his model for an age in which violence is mostly the work of non-state actors. And by this, I mean to go even further than the brutal critique by John Keegan I summarized above. It is not simply a question of jettisoning old ways, for there is still a great deal we can learn from the old Prussian for dealing with the likes of Russia or China or North Korea. We need to retain what works and improve upon or add to it for today's threats, at all times understanding the contextual limitations of all theorists and authors, no matter how famous.

Indeed, context applies to the other great strategist, Sun Tzu, who was also a child of his age. Why else the emphasis on victory without combat as the preferred goal? Unless we see Sun Tzu as a product of the Warring States period, before China was united, we cannot understand that his motivation was not to destroy the enemy, but to coopt the political entities that would become the building blocks of a new empire.

If the context in which Sun Tzu wrote was the drive for unity in China, the context for Clausewitz was the Napoleonic revolution in warfare and a young Westphalian system. *On War* is crucial to understanding the Westphalian period and the national security architecture to which it gave rise, but it has less to teach us about the post-9/11 age. As Martin van Creveld, one of the few modern strategists worthy of the title, has said, "What [Clausewitz] never imagined was a world in which many, perhaps even most, belligerents consist of non-sovereign, non-territorial organizations."

We must therefore ask some obvious but new questions to ascertain whether the old models apply. How Clausewitzian is the understanding of the purpose of war for those who wage irregular warfare against us? For example, is ISIS, or even Iran, driven by the same functional approach to the use of violence as we are? *On War* may remain the key text for nation-versus-nation conflict, with actors operating on logical cost-benefit lines directly connected to obvious political gains. But is the same calculation behind the violence of a religiously-motivated foreign-fighter brigade in Iraq, a Taliban militia in Afghanistan, or a jihadist mowing down innocent Americans in an Orlando night club?

Clausewitz was right about the immutable nature of war, but his Westphalian context shaped his understanding of the role of *raison d'état* and the trinity of forces that the state both embodies and leverages. Those forces still exist, but the new actors we face—whether they be the Taliban in Afghanistan or surviving al-Qaeda units in Yemen—make very different calculations, in which rational, policy-oriented cost-benefit analysis and justifications are trumped or qualified by less dispassionate and more otherworldly influences.

The triangle of government, people, and army (or commander), representing, respectively, reason or policy, passion, and skill, is less than useful for many of the irregular threat groups we are fighting today because they are not nation-states. Take, for example, al-Qaeda, still quite active despite the media's failure to pay attention. Since the loss of its Afghan base of operations, no government or nation is associated primarily with this foe. The violence of al-Qaeda has no policy goals like those of a "normal" government. Its ends are determined by the religiously fueled visions of ideologues, some alive today, but many, such as Sayyd Qutb and Abdullah Azzam, deceased. None of these ideologues or irregular elites politically represented a nation in the Westphalian sense. The Clauswitzian trinity is simply not relevant.

Likewise, in an irregular army, the role of the military commander is not filled by a professional warrior subordinated to a political elite. Osama bin Laden was a self-taught warrior, a mujahid who never spent time at a war college or wore the uniform of a national army. Al-Qaeda's current leader, Ayman al-Zawahiri, was a medical doctor. His skill as a jihadi leader is not measured solely in terms that concerned Clausewitz, namely, prowess on the battlefield. Rather, he must be understood in non-military terms as an ideologue in his own right, an "information warrior" who inspires by personal example. The commander of the Clausewitzian trinity was judged by his ability to prevail despite the "friction" and "fog of war." Today's jihadist leaders, such as the head of ISIS, Abu Bakr al-Baghdadi, and jihadi operatives, such as the San Bernardino killers, are measured less by their success on the battlefield—minimal since 9/11—than by their "authenticity" as "true believers" and their ability to inspire others. Each is an example of a "holy warrior" prepared to die not for a political end state, but for a transcendental truth, judged by his capacity to inspire other violent non-state actors.

Finally, the passion and hatred-driven third part of Clausewitz's trinity must be redefined. No longer is the enemy limited by his national population. ISIS, like the Muslim Brotherhood, is not constrained by its ability to rally the citizens of a particular nation to the cause of war or by their willingness to be drafted into a national army. The enemy's recruiting pool is not based on a nation-state—it is global. Irregular warriors may be recruited from Algeria, Somalia, or Michigan. The population from which ISIS draws warriors is not territorially bound, but religiously defined by the idea of the *ummah*, or the global Islamic community. And in this, ISIS is not alone. The new anti-capitalist extremists and anarchists such as Antifa are also unrestricted in their mobilization by national borders. Consequently, although reports of the death of the nation-state may have been greatly exaggerated, a definition of war that pertains only to nations is indeed dead. Clausewitz's trinity still applies to state-on-state conventional war, but it must be supplemented with another trinity that can depict the types of actors our troops are already fighting.

Ideologues / Inspirational figures (Truth)

Global Sympathizers   Non-State Threat Group
(*Passion*)   (*Skill/Charisma*)

Figure: *The trinity of war for today's irregular enemy*

Clausewitz's trinity divided the world into three parts: the government, the governed, and the defenders of the state. Each reflected a different characteristic: reason, passion, or skill. Although the triangular representation of the three implies equality, it is clear from *On*

War that Clausewitz privileges the military, or more specifically, the artful commander, who harnesses the population's passion and might so the nation may realize its goals.

Today's irregular enemy should be understood as more egalitarian. Just as the media have been democratized, with websites and blogs turning consumers into producers and vice versa, the trinity of the irregular enemy affords and invites an interchangeability of roles and functions. Leaders can be fighters, followers can become leaders, and both can interpret and feed into the enemy's understanding of why force is necessary and what ultimate purpose it serves. In other words, the components of the Clausewitzian trinity have become utterly fluid and interchangeable.

This has profound implications for the resources the enemy can mobilize against us. We are faced by an Arab terrorist as the leader of ISIS, but the violence carried out in the name of the "truth" that he serves can be executed by a Nigerian "underwear bomber" on a commercial airliner or by an Uzbek terrorist turning his truck into a lethal weapon on a Manhattan bicycle path. There are no limits to who can be recruited and deployed against us. The only requirement is that they subscribe to the religious ideology that is global jihad, or to the next totalitarian belief system that justifies violence against anyone who disagrees with its adherents.

A second implication is that in the wars America fights today, national interest no longer governs the enemy's use of force. Rather, it is a truth defined not by a governing elite, but by ancient religious texts or the interpretations thereof by ideologues with both political and otherworldly motivations. Clausewitzian *raison d'état*, the objective of violence, is no longer bound by cold or technical definitions of national interest. If ultimate approval is promised to the religious or utopian suicide bomber or mass killer, then US national security elites must not assume that the rationale for violence is subject to the limitations of a Westphalian framework of analysis. In today's irregular warfare, therefore, we can replace the rationale of the trinity with the transcendental end that the true believers see themselves as serving.

Finally, in the new threat environment, the third actor of the Clausewitzian trinity—the commander and his forces—is radically redefined. During the early twentieth century and later during the Cold War, practitioners of irregular warfare had one very Westphalian goal: although they were not representatives of nation-states, they sought to seize state power. This is how the master of this kind of warfare, Mao Zedong, revolutionized our understanding of the utility of force. No longer was it strategically employed to serve an established government. Instead, by skillfully conducting multifaceted campaigns on diverse lines of effort, the insurgent could systematically build a "counterstate"—a shadow government that, when powerful enough, could challenge the incumbent in a conventional campaign, destroy it, and then become the new state itself. This is exactly what Mao accomplished in China with his "People's War," which broadened our understanding of warfare. But he also reinforced the Westphalian context since the goal of the insurgent was always to become the new nation-state.

Today, in contrast, we face a foe who rejects the state-centered Westphalian model, an enemy who is not interested in a war of self-determination in the classic sense of postcolonial independence. Instead, groups like ISIS and al-Qaeda fight for worldwide religious supremacy. Their idea of self-determination is tied not to the nation-state, but to a global theocracy, the Caliphate, within which all shall be subject to the will of Allah and not the will of the people.

It is likewise clear that the last element of Clausewitz's trinity must be reassessed in the case of an irregular threat group that is even more ambitious than Maoist People's War would have us expect. We cannot represent today's global jihadi movement as a nation-state military led by a commander serving national interests. This third part of the trinity is now populated by various types of actors. It consists of leaders such as al-Baghdadi or Zawahiri, who say they serve no government, only God. It also refers to domestic enemies such as Mohammad Sidique Khan, the British terrorist who masterminded the 7/7 London attacks. And lastly, it can also refer to the likes of Anwar al-Awlaki, the Yemen-based American Muslim cleric who may not have had classic command and control of Major Nidal Malik Hassan, the Fort Hood shooter, or Umar Farouk Abdulmutallab, the Nigerian "underwear bomber," but far more importantly acted as inspiration and sanctioning authority for both men and continues to inspire new jihadis from beyond the grave with lectures and videos that are still circulating around the globe.

WHAT DOES THIS MEAN FOR AMERICA?

Clausewitz is still valuable. His understanding of what war between states should look like has not changed with the arrival of a globally motivated and capable non-state actor using irregular tactics and strategies. Nevertheless, his trinity cannot be applied directly to such enemies. The context has changed. The world can no longer be described as consisting solely of the governed, the governing, and the regular militaries that serve them. It has become more variegated.

Fortunately, Clausewitz's other non-trinitarian insights into conflict still hold true. His image of a war as two wrestlers is as apt a depiction of Kennedy versus Khrushchev in 1962, and of Donald Trump versus Kim Jong-un today. This is the part of his work that we must reemphasize while deemphasizing and reframing his wondrous trinity. With an enemy who sees himself as divinely justified, the expression of war as a competition of wills is more important than ever. Clausewitz's emphasis on will over capabilities is doubly applicable today; it is the only way we can explain how untrained and pathetically equipped irregulars can challenge the best fighting force in the world despite its seemingly overwhelming technology and real-time intelligence.

If we have the audacity to update the Prussian master's trinity, we should perhaps renew our faith in his famous dictum while recognizing how much we have misinterpreted it of late. War may serve politics as its extension in the Westphalian way of doing business, but we should also understand that war is politics and politics is war. For too many years, the violence—the kinetic effect—has been our focus. Today, we face a foe who knows that war starts with ideas and depends on them far more than it depends on just weapons.

At the same time, the most significant threats we face today do not emanate from the world of non-state actors. They come from old nation-state adversaries who have seemingly learnt from the change wrought at the end of the twentieth century and who understand that the only way to defeat us is by using irregular and indirect means of attack. As our forty-fifth president has demonstrated, our military, when unleashed, can devastate non-state actors like ISIS. But they are not the only ones who have developed unconventional means to undermine our great nation. What have nations like Russia and China learnt about irregular warfare from our wars with al-Qaeda and ISIS? And how will they attack us when ready?

Eugene "Red" McDaniel

An American Hero Who Never Gave In

And now I knew the why of the suffering.
Now I sensed the purpose of my own Gethsemane
there in Hanoi—
I had to be humbled before I could know the perfection
Christ had in mind for me.
—CAPTAIN EUGENE "RED" MCDANIEL

*T*he human spirit is remarkable.

For those who have been blessed to be born in America and have never had to don a uniform and face down our nation's enemies in foreign lands, it can be impossible to fathom just what our brave warfighters have endured in the past and will again. Not simply the danger they face when flying over, sailing through, or marching across a war zone. But what it means to live the life of a warrior in a war zone. The isolation of being thousands of miles from home and loved ones, the physical exhaustion that comes when you have to stay awake not only to stay alive, but to safeguard the lives of those you have trained with, deployed with, and bled with.

But beyond all of these trials, there is the trial that begins when everything fails, when something you didn't or couldn't prepare for happens. When the routine mission leads to an end no one can imagine until he has lived through it. This ultimate test of the human spirit is the test of being a prisoner of war under the control of enemy forces who see you as less than human. This is the story of one man who lived and survived that hell for six years.

The Vietnam War may never be generally seen as an honorable chapter in our nation's history. The war came just as the counterculture captured the attention of America and challenged the traditional patriotic values of the 1940s and '50s, and those who fought it were doomed to be rejected and vilified by a large portion of their countrymen.

But the overwhelming majority of those who went to war—those who volunteered, and the many others who simply complied when their number was called—were honorable people. They went to protect us and the world, and however ignominious our departure from Saigon might have been, the sacrifices made by our men and women in uniform were not in vain.

I will never forget taking a group of young national security professionals to dine at the embassy of an Asian partner of the United States. The ambassador, in an eloquent address to an audience who had not yet been born when Saigon fell, told them with great feeling:

To many Americans today, especially young millennials like yourselves, Vietnam is considered to be the war that America lost. Not to me, my fellow countrymen, or the citizens of the free nations in Asia. By committing the blood and treasure of your country for so many years to the cause of stopping communism in Vietnam, despite the outcome for you, America guaranteed that my nation would never fall to the Marxists or Maoists. Communism died a political death in our country exactly because thousands of Americas died in Vietnam.

This is not the perspective of Howard Zinn, Michael Moore, or Oliver Stone, but that doesn't matter. Because they are wrong. That ambassador was and is right. His perspective, that of someone from the region, should lead us to reevaluate the role America played in Asia during the Cold War and to understand how beneficial it was for millions of people who were saved from the horror of communist takeover.

That said, the way we collectively treated our warriors during those years—including the government's incompetence in securing the release of those who had been captured and brutalized—is still a national disgrace. Here I share the story of one such hero, Captain Eugene B. "Red" McDaniel, a man who fought for freedom and was held as a prisoner of war, tortured for six years in Vietnam.[1]

McDaniel had flown eighty combat missions. Another twelve and he would be rotated off the USS *Enterprise* and sent home. But there was another "Alpha strike" to fly for the Joint Chiefs of Staff in his A-6 twin jet engine bomber. Another sortie deep into enemy territory to hit military targets in Van Dien, south of Hanoi, part of Operation Rolling Thunder.

The son of North Carolina tobacco sharecroppers, the six-foot-three thirty-five-year-old had served twelve years with the navy and was married to the beautiful Dorothy, who was back home looking after their three young children. This morning, McDaniel went through the usual routine before the pre-flight briefing. Ablution without aftershave or deodorant, on the off-chance his bomber was downed so the local forces couldn't smell their prey. Everything by the book. Except for the niggling feeling that today was different. Something was wrong. So much so that he couldn't even finish his usual eggs and bacon for breakfast. Was this the day? Would this be the mission that would end in his death? If it was, he found himself asking a strange question: Will my death be worthy of Dorothy and the kids?

Then it was into the cockpit of his plane, an airframe totaling sixty thousand pounds—thirteen thousand of which were bombs—that would be catapulted to flight speed off the deck of his home carrier in less than three seconds.

The mission was like all those he had flown before. As they penetrated deeper and deeper behind enemy lines into what was called "White-Knuckle Alley," the danger of being hit by surface-to-air missiles grew, and they "jinked" back and forth to confuse the radars scanning them for a sam lock.

But then it happened. The radar lock alarm flashed and the klaxon blared. On and on for an interminable twenty seconds until a Soviet-designed missile denoted in the sky between McDaniel's A-6 and his wingman. Shrapnel tore into his hydraulics, he lost control, and the plane headed into a nosedive. At two thousand feet, McDaniel ejected.

His parachute tore during the descent, and he crashed into the jungle trees below, coming to a violent halt forty feet above the ground.

Dazed and bruised, he climbed up the rigging of his trapped parachute until the branch it was caught on snapped. His fall badly injured his knee and crushed two vertebrae. And there he lay, with a pistol and a bottle of water, in a country where everyone around him wanted to kill any American he found.

Over the next two and a half days, hearing the whistles of the villagers around him who had been sent out to look for downed pilots, he tried to evade capture. Monsoon-like rain came and went, and he saw US planes searching for him and others who had been brought down. Out of water and covered with leaches, he waited for the navy to send a helicopter to airlift him before the Viet Cong found him. In desperation, he turned to the Lord, reciting the simple prayer of thanks his parents offered every night before dinner back home in North Carolina.

Red was the eldest of eight. His parents were people of faith but not regular church-goers; they didn't have the money to dress the whole family adequately, as they saw it, to honor God. In his freshman year at Campbell Junior College, Red found organized religion, and he became a deacon in a Southern Baptist congregation. Then he met Dorothy, whose father was a Baptist minister. Both the pastor and his daughter had a remarkable trust in God that was more sophisticated than his parents' simple belief in the goodness of the Creator. Red arrived at the understanding that Christ was real, a man of history. But more than that, the Son of God who had given of himself to all men, including Red. This understanding of God would be the secret to his survival of the horrors to come.

The rescue never came, and eventually, with the help of local villagers, the Vietnamese forces found McDaniel and took him prisoner. So began a six-year ordeal. They beat the dehydrated, injured pilot with rifle butts and struck him in the face as they led him on his painful march to Hoa Lo, the dreaded "Hanoi Hilton."

At the most infamous Vietnamese prison camp, the interrogations began immediately. Following his training and international law, McDaniel refused to share anything beyond his name, rank, date of birth, and service serial number. The first method of torture—the "ropes"—was simple and viciously effective. The prisoner was suspended by his wrists, which were bound behind his back, a position that placed a horrible strain on his shoulder sockets.[2] This position was held until the pain peaked. At that point, to exert maximum psychological pressure, before the next question was asked, the pressure would be released. If the pow offered no more than the legally required minimal answer, the torture was repeated.

Through it all, McDaniel resisted. He would bite down hard on the shoulder that hurt less to transfer the pain and attention away from the limb that hurt more. When the guards had walked away, he would do the same by banging his head against the wall, hoping to open a wound so blood would trickle into his mouth and relieve his burning thirst.

His Vietnamese captors pressed on, demanding that he divulge secrets about the latest US missile, where the navy would run its next set of missions, the strength of the deployed units—anything that could help them kill or capture more of his compatriots. The pain mounted and he lost control of his bodily functions, but McDaniel refused to divulge anything sensitive, pretending to go unconscious and then babbling seemingly important information that was in fact wholly fictitious.

After the first week, McDaniel had lost the use of his right hand from the repeated brutalization, and his right ankle had swollen around his iron shackles. By this time, the dreadful truth was clear: there was a great difference between Americans and their enemy. These people clearly enjoyed inflicting pain. For them, cruelty wasn't unusual. It was something that occurred against regulations when a unit that had seen too much horror succumbed to a collective psychosis and snapped. For the guards and interrogators of the Hanoi Hilton, this level of inhumanity was the norm, "standard operating procedure." This was simply what one did to an enemy combatant. And those who applied the brutal techniques of torture were not appalled by what they were inflicting. They liked to hurt their fellow man. Repeatedly. For days, weeks, months, and eventually for years.

And the brutality was not meted out only on the captive Americans. The Vietnamese prison guards reveled in maltreatment of animals. Pigs were deliberately blinded to make them more docile and controllable. Dogs, which were kept in the prison for their meat, were chased by their captors bearing clubs and bricks, until they stopped trying to escape and were killed, their meat now "tenderized" by the sport of chasing them. Sport was also made of dousing the numerous rats in the camp with gasoline, igniting them, and watching the rodents run until the flames killed them. Just for entertainment.

As the days progressed, McDaniel ended up in solitary confinement. Broken physically, he faced mounting psychological pressure as he tried to regain a scrap of strength, all the while hearing the screams of his tortured countrymen throughout the prison. Now the question became: How long can I hold out? When will I break? Because he knew worse was to come. He knew that what he had gone through was just his "baptism in torture." It was when he realized that it was it only the beginning that he started to pray, begging the Lord to give him strength in his solitude. After two weeks, the answer came.

McDaniel was escorted out of solitary to what he expected would be another round of relentless torture. Instead he was taken to a communal area. There on the floor lay a man, another badly wounded American. McDaniel felt sorry for him immediately, unmindful of what a pathetic and desperate sight he himself was. His fellow prisoner later told him, "When I walked in I looked like a man sixty-five years old [he was in his thirties], with boils all over my body, dangling right hand, left leg dragging from the knee, and stooped from my torture on the ropes."[3]

Nevertheless, McDaniel's prayer had been answered. Not only did he now have company, it was a friend, his fellow pilot Lieutenant Bill Metzger, who had been shot down just before McDaniel's plane was hit. But Metzger, supine and helpless, was clearly critically wounded, a massive shrapnel wound along one leg and his arms suppurating from multiple lacerations. That is when Red understood. Expending all his remaining strength, he picked up his friend and laid him on a plank bed. He had a mission—not from the Joint Chiefs, not from the Ready Room of his home carrier, but from God—to help his fellow man who was in an even worse state physically and spiritually than he was. He was there for a reason: to minister to those who needed him and who were unable to help themselves.

For the next three months, McDaniel ministered to his friend and others who needed his support, physically and spiritually. He realized that even when medical help was unavailable, a soul could be sustained and hope kindled. Communication was key. As prisoners were moved around and split up, staying connected to one another was crucial to maintain the morale to survive. Just knowing a friend was nearby could keep a man stay alive.

McDaniel and his fellow American POWs developed a matrix of five columns and five rows, one box for each letter of the alphabet (except K).[4] Tapping out messages to one another, prisoners could find out how the others were doing, rally spirits, or pass on news. Messages could be conveyed by quiet taps on a cell wall, the strokes of a broom sweeping a hallway floor, or the snapping of a laundered prison shirt being hung on a line to dry. Or just by coughing out the homemade Morse code when nothing else was possible. In this way, men kept their spirits up through the horror of the Hanoi Hilton—a horror that for Red McDaniel would last for years.

In his autobiography, *Scars & Stripes*, McDaniel explains not only how he survived the torture, depredations, and psychological abuse of those years, but also how he managed through it all to give to his fellow man, to help his fellow prisoners survive. He credits his mother, the sharecropper's wife, with showing him the way.

Mrs. McDaniel's optimism could never be broken thanks to her faith. Whatever the hardship, it was there to be faced, not denied or allowed to crush one's soul. "[T]he Lord would provide whatever it took to make it each day." And her son knew this not to be a empty slogan, but an article of belief that God could do anything. And so with faith in Him and in his Son, who made the ultimate sacrifice for all of us, there was no obstacle that could not be overcome. If He wants the highest good for me, the "the only way I could face each day [was] with confidence." Red learnt that at home, but it was an attitude that saved him and helped him save his fellow men through the years in captivity:

> If there was something to be lived in this sordid atmosphere of pain, then I had to live it. To abandon hope, the possibility of survival, meant I would lose possession of myself, my own worth, my own self-identity. In that case, the North Vietnamese had won—their intent was to destroy finally that sense of worth we all needed to hang on to.

McDaniel helped form a daily prayer club for the inmates. He would recite Bible verses he had memorized as a child, and the atheists and agnostics in the prison eventually joined them. The prayer club raised the morale of old prisoners and new captives, but worse was to come for McDaniel himself, including an extended period of solitude and the most brutal of tortures.

Some of the prisoners made a daring attempt to escape, communicating plans with the alphabet matrix during the weeks and months of preparation. McDaniel was not a member of the group that was attempting to escape, but when the plan was uncovered, he told his interrogators that he was, hoping to protect his fellow prisoners. What followed was the worst period of his incarceration, including electric shock torture. During these weeks, he moved beyond the simple optimistic attitude of his inherited understanding of God. Through his own suffering, he rose to a higher level of internalization, one made comprehensible by the suffering of Jesus on Calvary Hill. He faced the essential question: Had he truly allowed his Savior into his life?

McDaniel walked through that fire and survived. And for the heroism of his suffering for his comrades he was awarded the Navy Cross by a grateful nation.

The Vietnamese authorities mixed psychical abuse with more subtle psychological tactics, promising communication with loved ones or other concessions in exchange for the prisoners' participation in propaganda films intended to undermine American resolve. Some gave in, but very few. Their attitude of military professionalism boiled down to: "Ours not to reason why, ours but to do and (sometimes) die." As McDaniel writes,

> We believed in our commanders, in our President, and in the cause, no matter how marginal or confusing at times, and every military man since the beginning stuck by that and delivered the goods as best he could. I believed that what we were doing in Vietnam was right, that we were trying to contain Communist aggression. And even if the South Vietnamese didn't particularly care whether democracy or dictatorship ruled their lives, the point was that the United States was trying to draw the line here for the Free World.[5]

With that commitment to American values and faith in a God who will never betray his followers, Eugene McDaniel not only survived but helped others to survive. The citation for his Navy Cross begins:

> The President of the United States of America takes pleasure in presenting the Navy Cross to Captain Eugene Barker McDaniel (nsn: 0-1319/4751406),

United States Navy, for extraordinary heroism as a Prisoner of War (pow) in North Vietnam from 14 June to 29 June 1969. Due to an unsuccessful escape attempt by two of his fellow prisoners, his captors launched a vicious round of torture to single out the senior pows who were to blame for the breakout. During these torture sessions a confession led to exposing him as the communications link between the senior ranking officer of the main prison camp and the adjacent annex detachment. He accepted the responsibility for the escape and fabricated a story of his own planned escape. After interrogation, the enemy severely tortured him in their attempt to obtain information about the organization and policies of the American pows in the camp. Under the most adverse of conditions, he heroically resisted these cruelties and never divulged the information demanded by the North Vietnamese. His exemplary courage, maximum resistance, and aggressiveness in the face of the enemy reflected great credit upon himself and upheld the highest traditions of the Naval Service and the United States Armed Forces.

Shot down on May 19, 1967, Red McDaniel returned home March 4, 1973.[6] Reunited with his loyal and loving family, he once more proudly wore the uniform of a United States Naval Aviator and received the recognition of his nation and his fellow veterans. Returning to active service, he eventually became the commanding officer of the USS *Lexington*, retiring in 1982.

McDaniel resisted for six years as a prisoner of the North Vietnamese and kept faith with America throughout. As prison "chaplain" for the Hanoi Hilton, he prepared a sermon for his fellow patriots as they waited to be flown home to their families, basing it on the Old Testament story of Job:

[W]ithout labor no man can come to rest;

Without Battle no man can come to victory,

And the greater the battle the greater the victory.

CHAPTER 4

Winning the Next War: Know Your Enemy

You may not be interested in war, but war is interested in you.

—ATTRIBUTED TO LEON TROTSKY

*D*onald Trump inherited a dangerous world thanks to the feckless polices of the preceding eight years and the global vacuum resulting from President Obama's preference for "leading from behind." In a world of presidential "apology tours" and American "strategic patience," the real bad guys stepped into the vacuum so created and destabilized whole regions of the planet.

The world was on fire. Russia had invaded its neighbor Ukraine, China was aggressively building militarized artificial islands in international waters, Iran was charging ahead with its nuclear weapons program despite the mullahs's lucrative deal with the United States, North Korea was launching missiles over Japan, and ISIS had established the first caliphate since 1924. There were more than sixty-five million refugees from violence around the world, a number unsurpassed even during World War II.

Since Donald J. Trump took over as commander in chief in January 2017, however, American leadership has been restored. Have our enemies disappeared? No. But now we have the requisite fortitude and commitment in the White House to stand up for our values and take all actions necessary to protect our nation and its citizens. What should these actions be? You cannot defeat an enemy unless you know what he is thinking and how he plans to attack you. What follows is a primer on the three most important foes we face and how they are preparing against us.

THE WORLD DONALD TRUMP INHERITED

The United States' ongoing war against the global jihadi movement—which includes al-Qaeda, ISIS, and dozens of other jihadist groups—launched in October 2001 and is our longest formal military campaign since the founding of the republic. We have weakened the original al-Qaeda's operational capacity, and thanks to the sound leadership of the forty-fifth president, the Mesopotamian Caliphate of ISIS is just a memory. Nevertheless, the war is far from over as jihadists have moved to other regions, especially in Africa and Asia.

Nor has the jihadist threat in the West subsided, as the bombing of the Ariana Grande concert in Manchester, the London Bridge attack, and the vehicular massacre of innocent people on a New York bicycle path all too gruesomely attest.

At the same time, America's erstwhile enemy, Moscow, is acting with renewed belligerence. Its invasion of Ukraine broke the sixty-plus-year-old European taboo against territorial aggrandizement through force, and its fighter jet flybys of US vessels and along the American seaboard seem like a revival of Cold War era intimidation and brinkmanship.

The communist People's Republic of China, though it has yet to use direct force against its neighbors or the United States, has increased its military presence and strategic footprint through an array of unconventional means, from aggressive cyberattacks against US interests—both governmental and commercial—to the construction of artificial islands in disputed Asian waters.

None of these adversaries could expect to win a conventional war with a United States that still maintains a "hyperpower" position among the nations of the world. Therefore they are deploying old, unconventional techniques and developing new ones to progressively undermine our interests and weaken our allies and partners. We must study these techniques and find ways to counteract them before our national security is seriously undermined. The sooner the United States understands that the age of conventional warfare is past and that it faces irregular warfare from Russia, China, and "super-insurgencies" like the Global Jihadist Movement, the sooner it will be able to defeat or neutralize them.

HAVE WE LEARNT FROM THE PAST?

It has been said that history may not repeat itself, but it does rhyme.

The United States remains a true superpower, but mostly in one dimension: conventional warfare and kinetic direct action, such as the use of special forces and armed drones. As our nation's response to the war in Vietnam and the long conflict in Afghanistan and Iraq seems to attest, we do not much care for fighting "irregular enemies" in "messy" wars. This is a serious problem given that irregular warfare, as noted previously, is historically the prevalent mode of warfare.

At the beginning of our second decade fighting the jihadists, the Joint and Coalition Operational Analysis division of the Joint Staff at the Pentagon published a set of reports under the title *Decade of War: Enduring Lessons from the Past Decade of Operations*. Several of the observations and conclusions concerning Operations Enduring Freedom and Iraqi Freedom bear directly upon current and future threats to our republic. They include:

- A failure to recognize, acknowledge, and accurately define the operational environment our units were deployed into, resulting in a mismatch between forces, capabilities, missions, and goals. (Preparing for war and understanding the enemy.)
- A slowness to recognize the importance of information and the "battle for narrative" in achieving objectives at all levels. (The role of the "intangible" and the will to win.)
- Difficulties in the integration of general purpose (conventional) and special operations forces.
- The exploitation by individuals and small groups of globalized technology and information systems to shape the battle space and approach state-like disruptive capacity. (The "downward democratization" of destructive power.)
- The increased state use of surrogates and proxies to generate complex unconventional threats.

There is widespread agreement among those who have been responsible for planning and running our more kinetic operations since 9/11 that, on the whole, our armed forces have performed without peer in the application of direct force. America's ability to execute "strike and maneuver" missions has developed to such a degree that no other nation can come close to our capabilities in the conventional and special forces domains.

But when we have stepped beyond the application of "steel on target" and moved into the indirect and unconventional domains, we have rapidly lost our peer position to others who have devoted more time and thought to these less obvious modes of attack. ISIS had a force less than ten percent the size of ours, yet managed to bring the jihadi way of war to our shores more frequently than ever before, despite losing its main base of operations in Iraq. China now escalates its military adventurism daily according to its "One Belt, One Road" strategy: a plan to displace us as a global power. And recently, the Russian Federation has not only employed established modes of irregular warfare in Europe in ways that would impress even surviving members of America's original irregular warfare organization, the OSS, but deployed a full suite of information operations (IO) techniques in the Middle East, Europe, and even the United States which match anything from the heyday of the USSR.

What follows is the minimum we must know about our adversaries' unconventional and irregular techniques—the bare essentials for a better understanding of the ways America will be challenged.

THE MODERN WAY OF JIHAD

The modern movement for global jihad was born with the Muslim Brotherhood in Egypt after World War I, refined by the fatwas of the jihadi strategist Abdullah Azzam, and brought to spectacular international prominence by Osama bin Laden and the attacks of September 11, 2001.[1] But in recent years, the global jihadi movement has been transformed. After the death of bin Laden and the separation of al-Qaeda in Iraq from its parent organization, ISIS became the new standard bearer for holy war against the infidel in ways that made it far more dangerous than al-Qaeda ever was.

After the collapse of Syria, the jihadi capture of Mosul, and the multiple ISIS-connected attacks around the world, including the San Bernardino and Orlando massacres, people almost forgot about al-Qaeda and its leader, Ayman al-Zawahiri. And for good reason, for on at least four counts, the Islamic State had become more powerful than al-Qaeda had been. First, unlike al-Qaeda, the Islamic State was a true insurgency. Second, it became the richest non-state threat group of its kind. Third, it demonstrated stupendous recruitment capabilities. And most importantly, the Islamic State achieved that which all other modern jihadi groups have failed to achieve: the reestablishment of a theocratic caliphate.

Wherever al-Qaeda operated after 9/11, it never did so as a true insurgency. Instead it maintained its identity as a globally ambitious and operational terrorist organization. Even when it collaborated with a local insurgency, as in Somalia and Afghanistan, it did so parasitically. True insurgencies, like al-Shabaab and the Taliban, have a mass base of support and so many fighters that they can operate openly in daylight, capture territory, and hold it. Regular terrorist groups are by nature much smaller. Lacking a mass base of support, they must operate covertly. They hide in safehouses when inactive or plotting. They rapidly execute an attack and return immediately to their hiding place. An insurgency, on the other hand, functions as a quasi-military force. It can muster recruits and deploy them in formation, not just to attack, but to exercise lasting control over the territory it captures. For the insurgent, violence is but one tool with which to challenge government writ. For the terrorist organization, which has no true military capacity, violence is reduced to a means of coercion; a messaging platform for intimidation.

Al-Qaeda was never a true insurgency. Even in Afghanistan and Somalia, where it was linked to an insurgency, it never recruited its own mass base of support, piggy-backing instead on pre-existing insurgencies such as the Taliban and al-Shabaab. ISIS became all the more impressive because it took no shortcuts to quasi-statehood. ISIS wasn't just another terrorist group perched upon another pre-existing insurgency. It didn't have to borrow its fighters from another, older threat group. ISIS recruited its own mass base of fighters—more than eighty thousand in a few years. ISIS become more powerful than al-Qaeda because it grew into a true insurgency, the first modern insurgency of its kind.

One characteristic unites all modern insurgent groups. Be it Mao Zedong in China after World War II or the FARC in Colombia in the 1980s, and whatever its ideology, they all share a proximate goal: the defeat and displacement of the government they are fighting. Mao wanted to defeat and replace the nationalists and establish a Marxist

China. The FARC wanted to defeat and replace the Hispanic elite of Bogotá and establish a Bolivarian people's republic. Whether they were in Asia, Latin America, Africa, or Europe, insurgents were classically set on replacing just one regime: the regime with which they were at war. The Islamic State was far more ambitious.

Having built its own insurgent base with tens of thousands of fighters, ISIS went on to distinguish itself in four important ways. First, it managed to capture city after city in Iraq, Syria, and Libya; the first insurgency to control land in multiple countries in one region. On top of that success, it spread into West Africa, where Boko Haram, the Nigerian jihadi group, swore *bayat*, the Arabic pledge of allegiance, to Abu Bakr al-Baghdadi, the caliph of the Islamic State. Boko Haram was accepted into the new "caliphate" under al-Baghdadi's leadership and changed its name to the West Africa Province of the Islamic State, meaning that any territory under its control was a de facto part of the sovereign Islamic State. Never before had an insurgency captured and held land in multiple nations of multiple regions. In this case, the Middle East and North and West Africa.

Second, the Islamic State became the richest threat group of its type ever seen. Unclassified government estimates put its income at two to four million dollars per day, which accord with the *Financial Times'* estimate that ISIS achieved an "insurgent GDP" of five hundred million dollars. Considering that the 2001 attacks on New York and Washington cost al-Qaeda only five hundred thousand dollars,[2] ISIS had advanced to a completely different league from its progenitor's. It was in no way a "JV team," as President Obama would have had us believe.

Third, the Islamic State was incredibly impressive at mobilizing jihadist fighters. In the first nine months of its renewed operations in Iraq, ISIS managed to recruit nine thousand fighters. In the past few years, it has recruited more than eighty-five thousand men, at least thirty-five thousand of whom have come from outside Iraq and Syria. Given that al-Qaeda, operating as the Arab Services Bureau for

Mujahideen, recruited only fifty-five thousand fighters during the entire Afghan war of 1979–1989, ISIS has proved itself a far more impressive—and deadlier—organization than al-Qaeda.

The fourth, and most important, way in which the Islamic State truly stands out is by ruling a substantial territory. When Abu Bakr al-Baghdadi proclaimed the rebirth of the caliphate—the theocratic Islamic empire—from the Grand Mosque of Mosul on June 29, 2014, and proceeded to exercise true control over a population of more than six million in a territory larger than Great Britain, he achieved what no other jihadist group had in the past ninety years.

Here it is crucial to remember that the caliphate is not just the fabulist whim of religious extremists, but a political and religious reality that reigned for more than a thousand years. Established in Mecca and based over the centuries in Damascus, Baghdad, and Constantinople (modern-day Istanbul), the caliphate existed until just a hundred years ago in the form of the Ottoman Empire. Mustafa Kemal Atatürk, head of the new Republic of Turkey, which supplanted the empire after World War I, was intent on secularizing his nation and officially dissolved the caliphate in 1924. Jihadists have been trying to bring it back ever since, starting with the Muslim Brotherhood, founded in 1928. Hundreds of extremist organizations, including al-Qaeda, sprang up over the next nine decades with the express purpose of undoing what Atatürk had decreed. Yet, every one of them failed. The Muslim Brotherhood won the presidency of Egypt in 2011, but it tried to Islamize the nation too rapidly and blatantly, provoking a military coup and the restoration of secular rule in 2013.

The question is, how exactly did ISIS succeed where all the other jihadist groups had failed? American forces under the command of President Trump may have managed in 2017 to dismantle the new caliphate in short order, but it could be rebuilt elsewhere. Will a post-ISIS group succeed in a new region, such as Africa or Asia? The answer to how ISIS built its Islamic State is twofold, and we must understand it if we are to vanquish the Global Jihadist Movement and prevent its next insurgency.

The first of ISIS's secrets was leveraging a religious narrative, specifically an eschatological one that portrays its holy war as the "final jihad" before the end times. Abu Bakr used Islamic prophecies that the final judgment will be preceded by a series of mighty conflicts, the last of which will take place in the land of al-Sham—"Greater Syria," or Mesopotamia—the birthplace of ISIS. Thus, the message to all who were inspired by the jihadi attacks on and after 9/11 and who wanted to guarantee eternal salvation for themselves as *mujaheed*, jihadi martyrs, was incredibly powerful:

> "We are fighting and winning in a jihad on the territory
> that you have been told is the site of the very Last Jihad.
> You will have no opportunity to be a holy warrior after this
> jihad, for we are on al-Sham, and this is the last war against
> the infidel before Judgement Day. Come now or not at all."

This is how Abu Bakr and ISIS managed to recruit tens of thousands of fighters so rapidly and inspired dozens and dozens of attacks in the United States and Europe.

The second secret of ISIS's success has to do with an Egyptian jihadi theorist of irregular warfare.

THE JIHADISTS FIND THEIR MAO

Prior to the success of the Islamic State, the key strategists of the Global Jihadist Movement were less than pragmatic. The majority saw violence as a sacred act with the fate of their movement wholly contingent on the will of Allah. The holy warriors of Allah would execute violence against the infidel in an escalation of operations until the caliphate was miraculously established.

This idealistic attitude was challenged in 2004 when the Egyptian Abu Bakr Naji published *The Management of Savagery* on the internet. Although Naji was killed not long afterwards, he provided the Jihadist Movement with a much deeper understanding of irregular warfare than it had before. *The Management of Savagery* is a very dangerous book.

Like all jihadis, Naji believed that a Muslim must live under a caliphate and that war must be waged until the Empire of Islam covers the world. He makes it clear, however, that violence alone will not produce a functioning caliphate. Instead, the jihadi movement must follow a comprehensive plan of operations that will bring about the desired theocracy in stages. Naji describes three operational phases.

Phase One is *vexation*. In the initial stage, the jihadist organization will wage irregular warfare, executing dramatic terrorist attacks against the infidel and his regional partners. The goal here is to weaken the infidel and apostate partner governments and prepare the battle space for the next phase.

Phase Two is *spreading savagery*. The jihadist organization steps up its irregular warfare, drastically increasing the size and frequency of its attacks. The objective of Phase Two is to dislocate the local government, making it impossible for the Syrian government or the administration in Baghdad, for example, to exercise true sovereign control over its territory. The chaos becomes so bad that the population loses faith in the existing government and comes to accept the insurgents, vicious though they may be, as a preferable alternative.

Phase Three is *administer savagery, consolidate, expand*. Now, the insurgents consolidate their control of captured territory ("hold and build"). Members of the local population are integrated into new fighting units. A new governance structure is put in place, wedding the provision of services with imposition of a draconian system of justice based on sharia law. The captured territory is gradually converted into a new "base state" that can be used as a launching platform for Phase One and Phase Two operations in new territories—Libya and Yemen, for example—continuing the expansion of the caliphate.

The significance of Naji's work is that it gave the global jihadi movement a measure of pragmatism and a real understanding of irregular warfare that had been missing for ideological and theological reasons. Phase Three is really a transitional stage, after which the final global caliphate will be achieved, a period when the jihadist enterprise is functioning as a quasi-nation-state with a fixed territory, administration, and monopoly of force. Earlier jihadi strategists had rejected the Westphalian nation-state as a heretical construct of the infidel West. Naji's great contribution—and a very dangerous one—was to argue in *The Management of Savagery* that even if one doesn't like the nation-state conceptually, it is an evolutionary stage through which the movement must pass if it is to serve Allah by re-establishing his Islamic Empire. And Naji's pragmatic approach was effectively implemented by Abu Bakr and his Islamic State jihadists during President Obama's second term, especially after his disastrous decision in 2011 to withdrawal our troops from Iraq.

Since President Trump assumed command, the United States and its local partners have been remarkably successful in taking the fight to the new Islamic State. But the war is far from over, and other jihadists may follow Naji's strategy to destabilize other parts of the world important to America.

WAR BY OTHER MEANS: THE SOVIET UNION IS DEAD, LONG LIVE THE RUSSIAN FEDERATION

Today's Russia may not be the Soviet Union. It is not an existential threat to the United States. But it is an anti-status quo actor and a spoiler controlled by a thuggish former KGB officer who called the dissolution of the USSR the "greatest geostrategic calamity of the twentieth century." Moscow is therefore committed to re-establishing its unchallenged dominance in Central and Eastern Europe and beyond. Its invasion of the sovereign nation of Ukraine and the annexation of Crimea were masterly demonstrations of how to conduct irregular warfare in a post–Cold War and post-9/11 world. Its exploitation of the vacuum left by the withdrawal of American combat forces from Iraq in 2011 shows how ambitious the Kremlin is to reshape the geopolitics of the Middle East as well.

How has Russia done this? Some have argued that it has developed a new mode of "hybrid war." This is not true. Moscow has simply further developed and recalibrated old Cold War tools, employing them in a way that emphasizes a less direct and more subversive approach to war that Sun Tzu would have instantly recognized.

Some of the most important work showing the world how Russia is winning its wars without recourse to conventional means is coming from the Baltic nations of Estonia, Latvia, and Lithuania, which are under the greatest threat since the invasion of Ukraine. The best English-language summary of the revamped Russian approach to war can be found in the 2014 report of the National Defense Academy of Latvia's Center for Security and Strategic Research. Titled *Russia's New Generation Warfare in Ukraine: Implications for Latvian Defense Policy*, it identifies eight ways the Russians are adapting their strategy for conflict in the twenty-first century:

- From direct destruction to direct influence. From direct conflict to "contactless war."
- From direct annihilation of the enemy to subverting it internally.
- From war with kinetic weapons and an emphasis on technology and platforms to a "culture war" attacking the will of the enemy.
- From war built around conventional general-purpose forces to sub-conventional war using special forces and irregular groupings and militias.

- From the traditional three-dimensional perspective of the battle space to an emphasis on information operations, psychological operations, and the "war of perceptions."

- From compartmentalized war to a "total war," including the targeting of the enemy's "psychological rear" and population base.

- From war focused on the physical environment to war targeting human consciousness, cyberspace, and the will of the enemy to fight.

- From war in a defined period to a state of "permanent war." War as the nation's natural state.

The Russians implemented these new strategies in Ukraine, which was subverted politically, psychologically, and economically before any hostilities broke out. The Latvian report describes eight clear phases in the subversion of Ukraine:

Phase One: *Non-military unconventional warfare* encompassing informational, moral, psychological, ideological, diplomatic, and economic measures supporting the overall Russian plan to establish a political, economic, and military environment favorable to the interests of Moscow.

Phase Two: *Special operations* designed to mislead the adversary's political and military leaders, including the leaking of false information and counterfeit orders to diplomatic channels, the media, and key government and military agencies.

Phase Three: *Subversion.* Intimidating, deceiving, and bribing adversarial government personnel and military officers with the objective of making them abandon their official and service duties.

Phase Four: *Propaganda and information operations* targeting the civilian population to increase discontent amplified by the arrival of Russian-sponsored and trained bands of militants, escalating subversion.

Phase Five: *Military measures below open war,* including the establishment of no-fly zones, blockades, extensive use of unconventional war units and direct action in close cooperation with armed "opposition" units.

Phase Six: *Open use of force.* The commencement of military action, immediately preceded by large-scale reconnaissance and sabotage missions. Employment of all means of attack and all types of assets, kinetic and non-kinetic, including special forces, space capabilities, electronic warfare, aggressive and subversive diplomacy, intelligence assets, industrial espionage, allied force-multipliers, and embedded fifth-column actors.

Phase Seven: *Force escalation.* The intensification of targeted information operations, increased electronic warfare, air operations, and harassment, combined with the use of precision weapons launched from multiple platforms, including long-range artillery and the use of weapons platforms based on new physical principles such as microwaves, radiation, and non-lethal biological weapons targeting the enemy's will to resist.

Phase Eight: *Assert control.* Roll over and neutralize all remaining resistance, use special forces and stand-off platforms to destroy remaining combat-effective enemy units, deploy airborne assets to surround the last points of resistance, and execute "mop-up" and territorial control operations with ground forces.

None of these measures constitutes a new type of war. It is the focus and combination of modes of attack that have changed. Moving away from the Cold War scenario of all-out war—including the deployment of chemical, biological, and nuclear weapons—and *maskirovka* (deception) and making indirect and non-kinetic conflict a priority, the Kremlin has adapted Sun Tzu to our time. The perfect victory is to win without fighting *too much.*

The Russians will continue to employ subterfuge, subversion, and indirect attack. Russia does not share America's interests. It may face its own jihadi threat, especially from Chechnya, but that does not mean it is, or can be, our friend. Vladimir Putin built his career in the KGB on denying the God-given rights of his fellow man and undermining the national security of America. That is why he has publicly lamented the loss of the Soviet Union as a tragedy. Not the gulag. Not the forced starvation of millions of kulak farmers. Not the torture of thousands in the bowels of the KBG headquarters of the Lubyanka. No, not that, but the loss of the system that was responsible for all that death and suffering—that was the tragedy for the King of the Kremlin.

Russia is not our friend. We need to know it and prepare to neutralize it when it endangers our vital interests. But there is another foe we face, and unlike Russia, it is rising in power. It intends to undermine us and replace us as a global force for good.

Let us now look at China.

THE NEW SUN TZUS: "MAKING TROUBLE FOR THE TROUBLEMAKERS"

Shortly before 9/11, two senior colonels of the Chinese People's Liberation Army, Qiao Liang and Wang Xiangsui, men with experience in political warfare, published *Unrestricted Warfare*, an argument that drastic changes in the context of conflict require a "new" type of war without limits.

Qiao and Wang focus first on the geostrategic and geopolitical changes that necessitate unrestricted warfare, discussing globalization, the waning power of the classic nation-state, and the rise of "super-empowered" actors such as hackers and cyber warriors. The authors offer a lengthy discourse on the significance of the First Gulf War in demonstrating the new "omnidirectionality" of combat and enumerate the eight principles of unrestricted warfare:

- *Omnidirectionality*: A 360-degree perspective guaranteeing consideration of all the factors related to war. The goal is to eliminate blind spots when observing the battlefield, designing plans, and employing measures. Warfare can be military, quasi-military, or nonmilitary, and the "battlefield" exists everywhere with no distinction made between combatants and noncombatants.

- *Synchrony*: Conducting actions in different locations at the same time. Synchrony accomplishes objectives rapidly and simultaneously.

- *Limited objectives*: Limit objectives in relation to measures employed. Objectives must always be smaller than the measures used to obtain them.

- *Unlimited measures*: Once objectives are limited, there should be no restrictions placed on the measures used to achieve them. Hence "unrestricted warfare."

- *Asymmetry*: Understanding and employing the principle of asymmetry correctly so as to find and exploit an enemy's weaknesses.

- *Minimal consumption*: Using the fewest combat resources necessary to accomplish the objective. The analogous principle in the US military is "economy of force."

- *Multidimensional coordination*: Coordinating and allocating all forces that can be mobilized in the military and non-military spheres covering an objective, including non-military assets such as cultural warfare.

- *Holistic adjustment and control of the entire war process*: Continual acquisition of information throughout the campaign to allow for iterative adjustment and comprehensive control.

As even a cursory glance will demonstrate, none of these principles are at all new. Several are as old as *The Art of War* itself. Others are simply common sense. Nevertheless, we shouldn't disregard this work, or rather, we shouldn't conclude that there is nothing new in Chinese thinking about war, the exercise of power, and how it can oppose American interests.

Every nation—and even every non-state actor—has its unique strategic culture. China's has been shaped primarily by its experiences in two quite different epochs: the original period of the Warring States, which produced Sun Tzu, and the nineteenth and early twentieth centuries. The former epoch left China's generals and leaders with an obsessive concern for maintaining internal cohesion. The latter left the political elite determined that China should never again be exploited and humiliated by foreign, especially Western, powers as it was for so long in the modern age.

What, then, are China's strategic goals? Qiao and Wang may not have expounded a revolutionary new doctrine of war for their nation, but Beijing is most definitely practicing a shrewd form of irregular warfare, less aggressive, perhaps, than Russia's in that its primary purpose is not subversion, but intimidation and economic control.

Simply looking at China's actions in Latin America and South Asia, where it has "invested" billions in countries like Venezuela and Afghanistan for access to natural resources such as oil and copper, we see how China uses the non-kinetic to realize its national goals. The privatization and cooption of the state that China has perpetrated in, such African countries as Angola and Nigeria, show how global an actor China has become in recent years. Russia subverts and buys individual actors. China buys the good will of whole governments in ways that are reminiscent of the mercantilism of the West a couple of centuries ago. In short, Beijing's approach is to exploit weak nations and corrupt regimes as well as the weaknesses of strong nations. As for the strongest of its competitors, the United States, Qiao Liang, told an interviewer in 2012, when he was already a general, that the goal is "to make trouble for the troublemaker."

China wants to be the most powerful state in the world. To achieve that, it must dethrone America. If that happens, international affairs will be dominated not by a nation founded on the principle of "unalienable rights" derived from our Creator, but by a communist dictatorship run by a man who recently had himself made premier for life. Freedom-loving peoples cannot allowed that to happen. Fortunately, the current president of the United States understands the threat posed by Beijing.

WAR IS WAR: BACK TO THE FUTURE

As the empirical data show, war is most often "irregular" and "unconventional." Given America's capacity to maintain an overwhelming advantage in the conventional military arena, our adversaries will continue to develop and employ irregular modes of attack. Although not all of these are revolutionary, or even novel, they are already proving effective. The sooner our strategists and policymakers develop relevant counters and hone our own indirect and non-kinetic modes of attack, the more able we will be to secure our republic and ensure the security of all Americans and our friends.

Whittaker Chambers

One Man against the World

Not all heroes wear a uniform or carry a badge and a gun. Some are short, overweight, and desperately unhealthy civilians who nevertheless risk it all and are true heroes. This is a story about just such a hero.

It is said of Americans that we are a forgetful nation, that our historical attention span is short, that for us a century ago may as well be deepest antiquity, and that we have a reflexive disregard for the past that undermines our capacity to learn from the mistakes, trials, and victories of others. This is demonstrably true when it comes to our national experience during the Cold War, for the lessons we learnt then seem nigh forgotten just a handful of decades later.

One American who is owed a great debt by this nation but whose name is almost unknown among the younger generations is Whittaker Chambers.[1] He didn't fight our mortal enemies on far away battlefields. He was never wounded in combat or given a Purple Heart by a thankful nation. In fact, he was pilloried and vilified by the postwar ruling elite, accused of unspeakable things for one reason and one reason alone: he stood up to that elite and revealed the rot at its core. He gave the world incontrovertible evidence that the West was in mortal peril, that agents of a totalitarian ideology that wished to destroy or enslave us had reached the highest levels of the elite. But despite being ostracized and smeared, he stood his ground, faced these traitors openly, and wrote a book that remains one of the few truly life-changing works of its kind today.

Chambers was born in Philadelphia and grew up in Brooklyn and Long Island.[2] An abusive father and a psychologically unstable mother made his childhood particularly difficult, and he left home early, ending up as a manual laborer in the District of Columbia before enrolling at Columbia University, where he was recognized by his peers and professors for his sharp mind and impressive writing talent. At the same time, he found solace in the company of the Quakers, a spiritual people centered around a deep commitment to community.

In time, the idealistic Chambers volunteered for a Quaker mission to the Soviet Union, excited to be part of a team that would bring aid to those less fortunate than himself and his peers. But he found himself shunned by the Quakers when they read his earlier student writings in which he had extolled the virtues of being an atheist, writings that some even deemed to be blasphemous. The rejection by his new faith family deeply affected Chambers, who subsequently dropped out of college, a doubly demoralized young man who had finally found fellowship and recognition only to lose both.

Shortly after his decision to leave the life that had given him solace and a sense of belonging, his brother, Richard, committed suicide, sending him into a period of crisis. This was the moment when Whittaker Chambers searched for a mission, a vocation, a crusade that would allow him to crush a system that he thought deserved crushing—a system that had rejected him and made his brother end his life. Communism was the ideology that perfectly matched the young man's need to rebel. It became his new "godless religion," and he joined the Communist Party.

It was 1925, and Chambers saw in the fresh, new Soviet regime the model for sabotaging the ruling elite, bringing equality to America's shores, destroying capitalism, and building a society in which justice reigned.

At the beginning his activities were public, writing and editing for Marxist organs like the *Daily Worker*. But as awareness of the communist threat grew, so did the need for secrecy, and Chambers embarked on a six-year odyssey as a covert communist, a subversive agent of the international conspiracy that served the Kremlin and whose goal was the destruction of the West and democracies everywhere.

Chambers had one of the most important jobs: managing the secret lines of communication between the communist undergrounds in Europe and the United States. He eventually became the agent who transported the Kremlin's instructions to Soviet moles in the American government and collected the classified materials they had stolen for transmission to Moscow.

Whittaker Chambers shrewdly constructed a new place for himself in American society as an ostensibly patriotic, middle-class family man. After a few years of effective dissembling, he was rewarded with the enviable position of senior editor of *Time* magazine. All the while he was at the hub of Soviet spying in the United States and knew all the key spies and covert agents of influence.

But this mission would not last forever. Chambers was inevitably challenged by the reality of what Karl Marx's philosophy was doing to people who got in its way. First, there were the international reports of labor camps and the mass denial of the human rights and dignity of anyone deemed to be an "undesirable." Then came the vicious and deadly purges fueled by Stalin's paranoia, which resulted in the executions of thousands and thousands of human beings as "enemies of the state," not for any crime, but for being disagreeable to the the general secretary or his underlings.

This death toll was not restricted to the territory of the USSR and the slave nations in its iron grip. Otherwise loyal underground agents of Moscow, people Chambers knew personally, were suddenly kidnapped or simply disappeared from his network completely and were never heard from again. The paranoia also ended the lives of those who, like Chambers, had been most dedicated to the cause of communism.

This was when he realized that he knew too much. So capricious were the men in the Kremlin that he might be suspected of disloyalty or simply fall out of favor at any time. If that happened, he and even his family would be targeted. So in 1938, on the eve of World War II, Chambers took a momentous decision that would change his life, the lives of his loved ones, and the course of American history and the Cold War. He cut all ties with the communist network to which he had dedicated his life and went into hiding with his family. He left a treasure trove of documents collected from his covert assets with a relative to keep as leverage against any attempt against himself or his family. And in a desperate search for clarity about what to do next, he returned to prayer, asking for God's guidance.

As recounted in his remarkable autobiography, *Witness*,[3] Chambers had no intention of turning on his former masters and siding with democracy. He just wanted to disappear and protect his family from the NKVD (the predecessor of the KGB). But then, geopolitics intervened.

In 1939, Stalin and Hitler made a deal, the infamous Molotov-Ribbentrop Pact, whereby the Soviets and the Nazis agreed not to attack one another and divided up Europe between them. At this point, any lingering doubts Chambers had about the moral character of his former cause disappeared, and he could admit to himself what he had known deep down for so long: communism was an evil ideology that had led to the murder of millions since 1917 and was predicated on the crushing of the human soul.

Just as importantly, he finally understood his own culpability. He had personally assisted the most dangerous dictatorship on the planet and helped it kill those it saw as its enemies. It would not do, he realized, to stay in hiding. With the encouragement of a Soviet intelligence officer who had defected to the West, Chambers decided to share what he knew with the government of the United States. It was his first step down a path that would make him the most famous—and infamous—public witness to the threat of Soviet subversion of the American state. But his journey would be a long and painful one.

At first, the official response was nugatory, or at best, lukewarm. The bureaucrat he was introduced to at the State Department took the names of the Soviet moles that Chambers gave him and sent them all the way to the White House. But the West Wing showed no interest in this information, and the FBI, apparently preoccupied with the Nazi threat, failed to prioritize it. Meanwhile, the Soviet defector who had convinced Chambers to reveal the spy network was found dead in a Washington, D.C., hotel room with no fewer than three suicide notes next to his body.

Chambers' evidence of subversion at high levels, including the names of people in the communist underground with whom he had conspired, went unheeded for almost a decade, but when the American body politic finally awoke to the threat of Soviet domination, he was called to testify before the House Un-American Activities Committee (HUAC) in the first televised hearing of its kind in US history. One of the persons he identified as belonging to the communist underground of the late 1930s was Alger Hiss, a doyen of the East Coast elite.

A good-looking graduate of Johns Hopkins and Harvard Law School, Hiss had served in the Department of Justice before World War II and then in the Department of State. He was a central figure in the meetings that established the United Nations after the war and one of the highest ranking American officials at the Yalta Conference, shaping our negotiations with Stalin about the disposition of Europe after the war. At the time of the HUAC hearings, Hiss was still a member in good standing of the influential elite, serving as the president of the Carnegie Endowment for International Peace. The establishment rallied to his defense and two Supreme Court justices testified to his character.

Hiss denied that he was ever a member of the Communist Party, that he had ever known Chambers, and that he had ever done anything untoward in the interests of Moscow. His accuser—overweight, ill-kempt, and unhealthy—seemed thoroughly outmatched. Chambers was attacked day in and day out in the press, and Washington buzzed with the wildest rumors that he was a closeted homosexual, responsible for his brother's suicide, and even accused him of pedophilia. All of Hiss's denials under oath were destroyed when his lawyers made a fatal mistake.

Hoping to undermine Chambers' credibility and dig up evidence that would make Hiss look good and Chambers look bad, they sued Chambers for defamation, demanding all and any materials in his possession related to Hiss. HUAC subpoenaed all the documents, which included those Chambers had left with his relative for safekeeping all those years ago when he feared for the lives of his wife and children.

The evidence handed over to the committee included more than sixty-five pages connected to Hiss, many demonstrably typed on his own typewriter or written in his own hand, as well as confidential coded documents that Chambers could have obtained only from Hiss. This evidence proved that Hiss had been in contact with Chambers after 1936, which he had denied under oath. It also proved that he had been involved in espionage, but the statute of limitations on espionage had run. Hiss was charged only with perjury, convicted, and given a five-year sentence.[4]

The best way to understand the significance of what became known as the Hiss case is to read Chambers' autobiography, especially the introduction, which is framed as a letter of explanation to his children. It is also worth watching Hiss's and Chambers' testimony before the House to see both the polished Ivy League lawyer aggressively but smoothly lying and Chambers reluctantly bearing witness to the truth.[5]

For Chambers, this was much more than a personal story about friends who had betrayed their employers and their nation. This was a struggle for the survival of the civilization into which he had been born; a battle over foundational questions about man and God. Half the world said there was nothing above man, nothing beyond this earthly life. For Chambers, what was at stake was as transparent as the simplest of mathematical sums. Communism can exist only if there is no such thing as the human soul. If there is no soul, then anything may be done in the name of communism. And for a man who saw the existence of God in the beautiful intricacy of his infant daughter's ear, the response was clear: The "crux of this matter is whether God exists. If God exists, a man cannot be a Communist."

The sadness of Whittaker Chambers was the result of his belief that America was doomed to defeat. The Enlightenment had left the atheists and the worshippers of man's omnipotence ascendant. The West had lost confidence in itself, a confidence that was not at all lacking in the enemies of the Creator, be they Adam and Eve, who first placed themselves above God in the original act of disobedience, or the totalitarians in Moscow, who in the October Revolution had declared themselves God.

Nevertheless, Chambers never gave up. He bore public "witness" to the truth and the American ideal despite what he saw as impossible odds. And he did this knowing how he would be excoriated by those he uncovered and by the elite who would never believe what he had to say, yet could prove.

Whittaker Chambers was one man against the world, but a man on the side of the angels. His lesson must not be forgotten: the totalitarians claim a monopoly on the truth. Anyone who challenges them must be destroyed. In 1939, it was the Nazis and the fascists. From 1948 to 1989, it was the communists. Today, it is the jihadists and all those who wish to destroy us in the name of their ideology. America is defined by freedom, totalitarianism by its denial. Whittaker Chambers suffered for America, but for all the right reasons. He was, is, and always will be one of our nations heroes.[6]

CHAPTER 5

Donald Trump Won.
Is America Now Safe?

*I*t is clear that when General Mike Flynn described the election of November 8, 2016, as a peaceful "political revolution," he was absolutely right. The day America chose Donald J. Trump, a man who had never held political office before, to hold the most powerful position in the land, politics in the republic changed irrevocably.

We should remind ourselves of the situation then. The Democrats had a candidate who virtually owned the mainstream media: on the night of the election, the *New York Times* declared that Hillary Clinton had a greater than ninety percent chance of winning the presidency. She had spent $1.4 billion on a campaign in which she made it clear that she was entitled to become president because of her sex and last name. Nevertheless, a real estate magnate and reality television star defeated her.

How did that happen, and what does this mean for the future of conservative ideas? The answers to these weighty questions are not always clear. Donald J. Trump defeated more than a dozen establishment Republicans for the nomination, yet since becoming president, he has implemented policy after policy that would please the most traditional Reaganite conservative. Are we therefore safer? Are we better prepared to deter, and if necessary defeat, our adversaries? Can we finally push back on the political correctness that has hobbled us for decades? These are the most important questions we face today.

I have given hundreds of interviews over the years. Most are quite brief, frequently no more than three minutes. It is challenging, to say the least, to tackle large and strategically important issues when all you have is two hundred or so seconds! There are places, however, where one can really get into the substance of an issue or even open up in a more personal way about how one sees the world and thus provide deeper insight into the threats we face. One such platform is John Batchelor's radio show out of New York, an absolute favorite of mine, where I have been a regular guest on Thursday nights for almost a decade now. A show where the host has discussions with his guests that last for half an hour, sometimes a full hour. Similarly, Larry Elder's show and Dennis Prager's, and the rest of the faculty who have truly substantive programs on the Salem Radio Network.

But the most satisfying, meaningful, and personal interview I have had of late was with Dave Rubin of *The Rubin Report*. A former progressive, Dave calls himself a "classical liberal" with libertarian leanings. He has amassed a large following on YouTube and for his podcasts, in part, as far as I am concerned, because of his fairness, humble inquisitiveness, and natural ability to make his subjects open up on camera.[1]

He and I first met at a Turning Point USA[2] conference where I spoke on my time in the White House, the national security vision of the president, and the undying bond between America and the nation of Israel. Soon thereafter, I sat down with him for more than an hour to discuss the key issues covered in this book and to share my views on the significance of our nation's choice of Donald J. Trump as president, his role in America's rediscovery of herself, the rise of an utterly intolerant left, and the future of conservative thought.

Dave, who has an uncanny ability to focus an interview on the truly important issues, has graciously allowed me to reproduce our discussion for this book. It should provide you with confidence about our choice, a sense of security about our present, and a lasting sense of hope for our shared future.

> *The Rubin Report*: "Trump, Dangers of Political Correctness, and Foreign Policy"[3]
>
> **Dave:** We have already spent a good amount of time talking about *Star Wars*.
>
> **Sebastian Gorka:** Yes, I was very impressed, your green room and that poster. I'd never seen that McQuarrie poster before.
>
> **Dave:** That was the original 1977 poster. I wonder, do you think, because we're obviously here talking about national security and foreign policy and all that, do you think any of your thoughts related to foreign policy have anything to do with *Star Wars*? Because I do think at some level, some of the way I view the world has to do with some of the lore and all.
>
> **Sebastian Gorka:** I'm not sure it's cause and effect, but absolutely in terms of good and evil. I mean totally. The first three movies are about good versus evil before they become this social justice warrior absurdity. So yeah, sure, but as much as being the son of people who lived under Nazi and then communist dictatorship; these things kind of flow together.
>
> ● ● ●
>
> **Dave:** All right so you were in California because you were talking to a couple conservative groups here in

California. People don't believe that conservative groups could exist in California.

Sebastian Gorka: I don't live here, but I come in and out to do these events. Something is happening. Something is clearly happening. The energy I felt at the events here is like the energy I feel at events in Virginia or elsewhere, like Texas. And there's a commonality whoever you speak to, they keep mentioning the same things. They talk about the gas tax; they talk about sanctuary cities; they talk about the burden on businesses. When you get these things repeated enough times, you realize something is happening in California. Who knows where it will go but this isn't the state I used to call the "people's republic." I'm not so sure anymore.

Dave: Really? So do you think this could be something that could happen as soon as our next gubernatorial election that's coming up now? Or do you think that this is sort of long term maybe presidential election 2020 or ...?

Sebastian Gorka: All I'll say is the following: with the election of Donald J. Trump to president, the political rulebook has been shredded, burnt, buried, and then Donald Trump jumped up and down on it. It's gone, so any past expectations, any trend-lines are irrelevant. I mean, I traveled with the president, we flew on Air Force One to Youngstown, Ohio, back in June, and this is Steel Valley, right? This is the heart of the blue-collar, Democrat, manual laborers. We arrived at the stadium and the president was in the back. I was doing selfies with the crowd ....

Dave: You do love the crowd selfie. I have seen many crowd selfies with you.

Sebastian Gorka: Look! What does it cost me? They want a selfie? Yeah, sure, why not? So, I got to engage with these people, and I realized that in the stadium alone, twenty to twenty-five thousand people, everybody was either a former registered Democrat, or their parents, their grandparents were all Democrats. And then what happens when the president, when the First Lady Melania comes out on the stage? It erupts. The building erupts with chants of "USA! Drain the swamp!" And this is Democrat territory. Now if that can happen in Youngstown, Ohio, who knows what can happen in California?

Dave: Yeah, so I want to talk a little bit about your history and your parents and growing up that you just mentioned, but as long as we're on the first part of the Trump portion of this, let's just keep doing that. I heard you at the Turning Point USA event in December give a speech which was really wonderful, and you described Trump as the "icebreaker." And what I've been saying around here is that I view him as the bull in the china shop. We wanted a panther to knock over a few things, but we got the bull. I think that really is the same analogy that we're using there. So could you further expand on ...

Sebastian Gorka: Yeah, sure! So the United States was covered for at least thirty years in this massive permafrost layer of ice which is political correctness, and it had frozen over the media, education, politics, all of it, to the extent that by the Obama administration, the federal government was telling you who could use which bathroom. So just insanity. And then along comes a guy, who the first day I met him in June 2015 in his office in Trump Tower, the first thing I knew about this man is he's the kryptonite of political correctness. I mean, he couldn't care less about what the *New York Times* or CNN says about a given issue. So along comes this man to this layer of ice frozen over the country and *bam*! He slams into it like an ice-breaker and smashes through the ice. So he breaks a pathway for the nation to open up that sea lane.

And my argument to conservative audiences is that this is great, this is monumental. It wasn't going to be the panther. The panther could have never won. It had to be the bull. It had to be the icebreaker, but if you know your physics of ice breaking, you can send that thousands-of-tons'-worth of ship in there with its tungsten hull, and it rides up on the ice, slices through it. But if you don't have the flotilla behind it that comes up and keeps that passageway open, what actually happens? In real life, if you send one ship in, it breaks a path, almost instantaneously the ice comes around the bow and re-knits itself right around the ship and reseals. So this is the moment in the conservative movement where we have to get serious about what does it mean to be a conservative in the twenty-first century? What is the role of government? What is national security? Donald Trump is the catalyst. Now we have to do the heavy lifting of ideology and politics and policy.

Dave: Do you think he will, years from now when we look back, be anything other than the catalyst? How do you consider his ideas compared to traditionally conservative ideas? Because just in the last couple of months, after signing the omnibus bill, ... there's a big mess in Syria, we're not sure if there's going to be more intervention or not. He seems to be doing some things that are probably a bit more "big government" than perhaps you want, or than certainly his base seems to want. So where do you think he fits, actually, between catalyst and the flotilla?

Sebastian Gorka: First things first. I hate labels, personally. I think that labels are lazy thinking, and in the case of Donald Trump they're irrelevant. I'll credit Monica Crowley with this. The weekend after the election was David Horowitz's Restoration Weekend in Florida, which was either going to be a wake or the party it was. And Monica gave a great speech in which she said, "Look, everybody misunderstands who this man is. He was never an ideological candidate because you simply cannot put him in a box because of what he does. Whether it's his attitude to gay marriage. He's just a mixture. He was never an ideological candidate. He was an attitudinal candidate." And she nailed it.

Now what does that mean? Look at the last forty years. This guy is seventy-one years old. He's not going to change. He is who he is. What has he done for the last forty years as a professional? He's been committed to one thing: excellence. Whether it's a golf course in Scotland. Whether it's a skyscraper in New York. It's excellence, and all he's done is he's taken that concept and he's translated it into excellence for America once more. And that doesn't fit into neat, neoliberal, neocon, paleocon ... it just doesn't fit. He's about getting stuff done and being the best.

Dave: So how do you link that to what the general conservative movement is? I get what you're saying about labels, and I say it all the time. The labels now, especially because of Trump, the labels are all over the place at this point. The thing I'm struggling to fully grasp about the Trump thing is how does this connect to this huge split? You've got the Trump base and then you have the Never-Trumpers, and these people that should be kind of lining up, they can't get there. How do you connect those things?

Sebastian Gorka: You're never going to connect with the Never-Trumpers. The Never-Trumpers are pathological. I mean pathological. When Bill Kristol actually tweets out, "In a choice between the Deep State and President Trump, I choose the Deep State!" Bill, you're not a conservative; you're a subversive. Get out of the tent! So that's never going to happen.

The broader question of what does "conservative" mean today, we can't answer that. Have you seen a good article, a really good article, which understands first principles about what Trumpism is or what it should be? I haven't. I've seen a lot of people who think they know what they're talking about but who have never met the president. So I think there's a lot of work to be done, but it's not going to be done by conservative "establishment" individuals. The NRO [*National Review Online*] is not going to tell you who Trump is. And the NRO is not going to revitalize the conservative establishment. This is a new era. It's exciting, but we have to get to work to define what it means to be a conservative.

Dave: So that to me is why it seems so obvious that you're so passionate about this. That no one else was going to do it, and I think that's sort of what Monica was saying, and that's sort of what Horowitz has been saying for a long time, that no one else was going to break through. And now it's imperfect but at least there's some opportunity.

Sebastian Gorka: Let me be brutally candid. I grew up in the UK to Hungarian parents who escaped communism. I went through the private school system in the UK stiff upper lip and all that stuff, the debate club. So the president's style is not exactly the style I'm used to. I had to get used to it, and I understand why people have issues. The biggest thing people have issues with on the right are his tweets. I get it. But guess what, who was going to defeat Hillary? It wasn't Jeb Bush. It wasn't even Senator Cruz. None of them were going to. The only person who was going to cut through that miasma, who could break through the ice sheet of political correctness, was this rank outsider from Manhattan. Whether you like it or not, to say philosophically, he was the necessary but not sufficient cause of victory. You don't have to like it, but it had to be him with that style. We tried to do Marquess of Queensbury Rules for thirty years. Where did it get us? Where did it get us? Mitt Romney? Come on guys! It had to be Donald Trump. So now we have to backfill what this all means.

Dave: And that seems to be where I think you and so many of these other people that are part, or formerly, part of the administration, you had a very brief stint at the administration ...

Sebastian Gorka: Longer than some ...

Dave: Right. Years from now they'll go, "Wow! He was there for ninety percent longer than everybody else." But a pretty short stint, seven months. First, can you just tell me how you got involved—because you just mentioned you had only just met him a little before the election in the first place—and just sort of what happened that had you leave, because that will really tie into the media, which we are very much aligned right now.

Sebastian Gorka: So summer of '15 I got a phone call from a guy called Corey Lewandowski that I'd never heard of, and he said, "Candidate Trump is prepping for the big fall GOP presidential debate on national security. He'd like to talk to you." I said, "Sure." So I took the plane, flew to New York, and went to Trump Tower. It was just three of us in Donald Trump's office, and we had this incredible blue-sky discussion on national security issues, you name it, from the Civil War up to the Middle East to nuclear weapons, all kinds of topics.

Dave: How knowledgeable did he seem about things? Because this is one of the parts that people, that we have no handle on.

Sebastian Gorka: He's passionate, really interested. Not a guy you're going to debate what happened in Karbala in the ninth century, but really interested in this stuff and with opinions. Halfway through this discussion—and he was sitting closer to me than you are and Corey over there—and he does a classic Trumpism, he just stops the conversation and goes, "Corey, I like this guy! Let's hire him!" And that was it, and he asked me to help. I wasn't part of the campaign, but I became an advisor, wrote policy papers that he used in the debates, and we stayed in touch, but I never joined the campaign.

Then, as things progressed and the field whittled down to what it did, I kept meeting General Flynn at events. I was a participant, I was just in the crowd, and I kept bumping into General Flynn, and I've known him from when he was director of the Defense Intelligence Agency, and eventually he just pulled me in, and by October, the month before the election—I don't know if you're familiar with the system. In the presidential election, the last two runners get support from the federal government before the election, and they get offices near the White House to create "Transition Teams," to prep. So Hillary got one story and the [future] president got another story of this building. I was pulled into ...

Dave: That's hilarious. It's in the same building?

Sebastian Gorka: Oh yeah, and if you talk in the elevator, you were like, you had to ... [be quiet].

So I got pulled in and asked to work on the National Security Council Transition Team for General Flynn, and my wife, who has a background on the issues, was pulled in to work on the Department of Homeland Security team, and so I became a part of the official Transition Team. Up to the very last moment, the week of the inauguration, I was going to be doing counterterrorism stuff for General Flynn and the NSC, and then Steve Bannon, who knows me, reaches out at the last moment and says, "No, you're going to come and work for me in the office of the chief strategist as the strategist to the president." And that's how, you know, at 12:01 on January 20, I became the deputy assistant to the president.

Dave: So the second that happened, the media went bananas on you.

Sebastian Gorka: No, no, no. It's very interesting. They didn't go bananas until the "travel ban" dropped, and I realized things were not going well in terms of communicating the ban. So I said to Steve and I said to Sean [Spicer], "Guys, I've done a bit of media in the past. I can be the face of this stuff if you want." I mean we've got the NSC communications team, but I'm prepared to go on CNN and debate these guys. So they threw me into the fire, and I loved it, and the left went nuts. They just absolutely went insane. It was once I was vehemently representing the president on television that out came the hit pieces and the lies.

Dave: Yeah, let's talk about that a little bit, because I see this happening to anyone that I have any degree of respect for. I see it happen … and it's coming to me now too. I mean I see this happen to anyone who I think is trying to be somewhat honest. The endless attacks. There were just an endless slew of things, that you're an anti-Semite and all of this craziness. I mean at the Turning Point USA event that I saw you speak at, you gave one of the strongest defenses of Israel I've ever heard. But they almost take everything and do the complete reverse of it. What do you make of that tactic? Where it's literally the reverse of what the truth is. It's not just like, "We're going to take a line and make it seem a little different." It's "we're going to do something that's absolutely counter…."

Sebastian Gorka: You've got a big viewership. I know your "why I'm no longer a progressive" [Prager] video[4] has gotten, I don't know, millions of views now, so I'll open up a little bit, despite the size of your audience.

I have a reputation for being a scary dude and being a "hard ass," and that's fine. But after the seven months that I went through, and that my family went through, every time, every few weeks, I have the same emotional response, and it would probably surprise you or others.

As a human being, I want to try to understand how another human being who's never met me, who knows nothing about me or what my family has been through, can write what they wrote about me or say what they said about me.

It leaves me speechless that you can have such venomous hatred for somebody and peddle such egregious lies, and you not only call yourself a journalist but you actually think you're a human being.

I was attacked, and that's fine, because I'm a politically commissioned officer of the president. I'm a proxy. I was a proxy for Steve [Bannon]; I was a proxy of the president. I understand that. That's okay, but hey, why don't we debate the policies. They never wanted to debate the policies. It was ad hominem attacks and lies. And secondly, it's okay to attack me, but guess what, it's not okay to attack my wife, to attack my dead mother's reputation, and it's not okay to attack my teenage, high school–age son either. These people are reprehensible, and they're out of control, Dave. And they're not learning; they're doubling down.

Dave: So that's the part that I'm concerned about right now that people always ask me. I did an event in Irvine last night, and the question I'm getting more and more now is: Is this thing turning around? Now I sense that there is something brewing against it. There's something brewing finally, and I think anyone in this space, it's going to get a lot worse before it gets better, and that's what I'm concerned about. You're nodding already.

Sebastian Gorka: I think you're right. Under what conditions does something like that change? If we rule out violence. We don't want to have violence. The worst war we ever had was our Civil War with six hundred thousand Americans killed.

Dave: Even though they're subtly condoning violence.

Sebastian Gorka: They are. We see the CEO of Twitter is even condoning it. Let's pray to the good Lord that's not where we're going. So what's the other option? What's the other scenario? That they look in the mirror and they stop? But why would they? They reward each other for the lies. I mean look at *Time* magazine's latest issue. It's just a farrago of lies. It's all opinion pieces. It's not journalism. When you look at the people they celebrate at their get-togethers, they're not journalists. I mean there are maybe six journalists left in this country that are actually doing investigative research, like Sara Carter, like Mollie Hemmingway. When are they going to be recognized by the Washington Press Corps? Never. Never, because they don't comport with the narrative that we're Nazis and the president is a dictator. This is a man whose grandchildren are Orthodox Jews. Can you wrap your heads around it, *New York Times*, CNN, Huffington Post, Buzzfeed? You're reprehensible for calling this administration what you've called it. I know the president. It's not that he doesn't have a racist bone in his body; he doesn't have a racist molecule in his body!

The stunning thing—and this is why it was such an honor to work for him—the stunning thing about Donald Trump is—and, look, I have a Bible in my pocket. I can swear on it. I'll swear on this Bible. This man wants only two things for all Americans. He wants you and your family to be safe and he wants you to prosper. Which is what all American presidents should want, but you know what's stunning, Dave? He wants that for you whether you voted for him or not. He doesn't care whether you voted for Hillary. He doesn't care whether you wanted Bernie to win. He doesn't care whether you stayed at home and ate Doritos. If you're an American and you're living here legally, he wants you to be safe from harm, from gangs, from terrorism, and he wants you to prosper like he has prospered. This is the answer to your question: the left will never believe that, although it is true, and I can attest to it.

Dave: When they put you out there, and as you said you willfully went out to go for the ban, the Muslim ban, when we talked about it...

Sebastian Gorka: ...The *travel moratorium*. Don't fall into their narrative!

Dave: So we talked about it a bunch on the show. I did a bunch of videos. I've tried to be very fair. I have Muslim friends. I've had Muslims on the show and ex-Muslims, and I've had people that are critical of religion and people that are religious and the whole freaking thing.

Look, most of the most populous countries of Muslim people were not included on the list. The original list came out of the Obama administration and all that. So I tried to talk about it as fairly as possible, but it seems to be one of those issues. And then I think this will sort of lead us into your book as well. Talking about radical Islam and trying to make the distinction between Islam as a set of ideas versus Muslims as people, and of course you can't be prejudiced and all of that. This seems to be basically the stickiest thing we have going right now, right? Like it's just quicksand to even talk about it.

Sebastian Gorka: You mean the threat of jihadism?

Dave: The quicksand of trying to make the distinction. We have to be able to talk about ideas and why we have to fight for good ideas and against bad ideas but at the same time make sure that we're not being prejudiced against people and making sure that America remains the open, pluralistic society that it is.

Sebastian Gorka: Look, the argument in my book *Defeating Jihad* is a simple one. We live in the only country ever created on the principle of individual freedom and liberties, granted to us not by the government but by our Creator because we were created in His image.

The Founding Fathers said you have dignity because you are made in the image of the Creator, not because Washington says you have dignity. That concept of the individual's dignity and the freedom that it provides is antithetical to the spectrum of politics that says man is perfectible and perfection can be created. My first degree was in philosophy and theology, and I stated the issue at this event here in California.

All politics or ideological differences can be summarized in just two camps. It doesn't matter which country you're in or what era. Two camps: those that believe truth is objective and not man-made and those who say no, man can define truth and perfection can be created here on Earth. That statement that man can define truth leads to the gas chambers and to the gulags. Social justice warriors don't realize that they're walking down the same path, but it's the same concept to say, "I'm going to perfect the world, and there will be justice and equality." No you won't if we are free. There will never be justice for all and equality for all as long as we are free, because evil is real. Evil exists. Man is fallen. Jihadism is just the latest version [of that denial of objective truth].

My book is built on a simple argument. There is a connective tissue between al-Qaeda and ISIS and the Nazis of the Third Reich and the communists of the Soviet Union. Yes, they worshiped different things. One worshiped an Aryan race. One worshiped the working class. The other worshiped their version of Islam, but guess what the connective tissue is. They're all totalitarians, and if you disagree with them, guess what! You're going to be enslaved or murdered. End of story. And if you deny that reality ... and I've trained, I don't know, six to seven thousand federal officers. I've trained more than that in the military, when a military professional, an FBI agent, understands that his government is telling him what he can and cannot say about the threat group he's supposed to be protecting us from, then we have problems.

When President Obama says in 2011, writes a memo[5] to the chairman of the Joint Chiefs and the then attorney general, all counterterrorism training of FBI agents and the US military must not mention Islam and especially must not mention the word jihad, well that's like saying we're about to storm the Normandy beaches and we say, "Guys make sure your M1's loaded and your boots are tied up, but whatever you do, don't mention the word 'Nazi' because you could offend a German." It's a bad *Saturday Night Live* skit, Dave. It's insanity, and the fact that we weren't allowed to talk about it truthfully, that gets people killed. Political correctness eventually can lead to good people dying.

Dave: Yeah, that also explains why there's such craziness in Europe right now. It seems to me that we're going to consistently see the rise of right or far-right parties. But it really is just the symptom of not being able to talk about these issues honestly.

Sebastian Gorka: Let's differentiate between the rise of two different things. So we've just had an election in Hungary. We've seen elections in Italy and elsewhere, and we've seen Brexit. Let's not conflate two issues. There's a rise of very disturbing groups like Jobbik in Hungary. They're already crypto-nationalists and feed off a long-seated, anti-Semitic, kind of irredentist sentiment in the country.

Dave: So these are the true, sort of, they're not all white nationalists, but they're true, sort of, they want ethno-states and they, right?

Sebastian Gorka: It's complicated because there's history there. There's Trianon, there's Versailles, but they're bigots. Then you mustn't conflate that with the Trump phenomenon and things like Brexit's original causation. I don't even use the word "populism." I reject the word populism unless your definition of populism is: those kinds of politics that the "elite" disagrees with. That's a good definition of populism.

For me, this isn't populism. Trump winning or Brexit happening is a reassertion of democracy. I mean, why did Trump occur? Because people on the left and the right looked at D.C. and said, "You know, I don't know the difference between the Sunni and Shia, but, guess what, it's [US counterterrorism policy that's] broken. I don't know what a federal budget should look like, but we're spending like drunken sailors." So it's the reassertion of accountable politics vice faceless bureaucracy or "uni-party" swamp dwellers, whether they're in D.C. or whether they're in Brussels. So for me, we should welcome it with open arms. This is a reassertion of accountable government, but for the left that wants uniformity of thought and bigger government, it's "fascism."

Dave: So how then do you police that? I know you don't like that idea of policing and government coming in and fixing, but how do you make sure that the part you're worried about doesn't lead the good part because I think the left is always led now by its worst parts. Then that's why they purge everybody. In the video[6] you mentioned that I did on Prager U., that's what I talked about. Anyone that steps out of groupthink, you get purged, and that's why I think there's such a movement toward libertarianism or classical liberalism or whatever you want to call it. So I see what the left's doing on that. How do you make sure that doesn't happen on the right, where the far right that you're worried about ... you think it's fair estimation to call it far right?

Sebastian Gorka: I don't even like the word "alt-right." I think it's bogus. I think that's just a new label for nationalists or irredentist bigots. They're rewrapping themselves to be fit for polite company. They're just racists.

Dave: I hate to tell you on your Wikipedia page they call you alt-right, of course.

Sebastian Gorka: Wikipedia ... enough said. The page that doesn't allow the subject to correct mistakes. Right. When I try to correct the lies, it's frozen. That's interesting, Wikipedia.

Dave: I told you right before we started, but your Wikipedia out of all the ones I usually just glance there, not to get facts but just to get a sense, yours is such a mess it's ...

Sebastian Gorka: I've tried to correct it. Friends have tried to correct it. Then they froze it and then, forget about it.

Dave: So what do you do, though, to make sure those two things don't come together.

Where it all began: Trump Tower, New York City, summer of 2015, where the real estate mogul and TV star Donald J. Trump asked me for help in preparing for the Republican presidential debate on national security.

My worldview about good and evil and the perennial threat we face from totalitarians of all forms was shaped by my parents' childhood suffering under Nazi occupation and then communist oppression. This picture was taken in Britain not long after my father's liberation from a political prison in the Hungarian Revolution of 1956 and their escape to the West.

General Mike Flynn called November 9, 2016, a "peaceful political revolution," and he was right. A real estate billionaire TV star changed American politics forever, and at twelve noon on January 20, 2017, a handful of us who had been on the "MAGA express" with him officially started work for the forty-fifth President of the United States: Donald J. Trump.

On day one, I was flattered to be issued White House parking placard no. 6, allowing me to park on "West Exec." right by the entrance to the West Wing. But the boss still had a better spot!

One of the many surprises in the White House: just how small and unassuming the table is upon which the president publicly signs his executive orders.

The Oval Office is the Oval Office, but my favorite place to work of all on the White House complex was the old secretary of war's suite in the Eisenhower Executive Office Building, the original Department of Defense.

Making America Great Again is not about one man or one election. It's about returning the greatest nation on God's earth to its founding principles. Here, with a young Conservative during the president's trip to Youngstown, Ohio.

There may have been perks, but we worked hard for the "big bucks"! I would try to be in the West Wing soon after seven o'clock most mornings, and it wasn't unusual for us to see the sun set over the People's House, which could be utterly beautiful.

The infamous whiteboard from the office of Steven K. Bannon, chief strategist to the president, where we tracked promises Trump had made and checked off our accomplishments at a speed other administrations would have been jealous of.

"Fake News" is real, and President Trump pushes back on the lies and distortions every day, but he is not alone. Here, my colleagues from the National Security Council and I meet with friendly journalists to provide background on what the president has planned for the Middle East and how ISIS will be defeated.

America's helm: Just across the hall from the Oval Office is the Roosevelt Room, where the president hosts his guests and where his advisers hold formal meetings below the cabinet level. A rather romanticized bust of our first president rendered in the Roman style stands vigil outside the door.

One of the great pleasures of working in the center of power is the people you spontaneously meet. In this case it is Rabbi Uri Pilichowski, visiting the White House from Israel with a group of high school students. The rabbi and I immediately clicked, and I value his friendship to this day.

The proudest moments of my tenure were when the president reasserted the interests of the American people over the interests of other governments and international lobbies. On June 1, 2017, I stood at the back of the Rose Garden as he told the world, "I was elected to represent the citizens of Pittsburgh. Not Paris." And with that, we left the Paris Climate Accord, which had penalized Americans while countries like China and India continued to pollute and receive our cash subsidies. Making America Great Again wasn't just a campaign slogan. It is the president's mission statement.

The new first family brings a bygone level of dedication and style back to the White House. With Ivanka in the Roosevelt Room just across from her father's new office.

David Friedman has worked for and been a friend to Donald Trump for a very long time. It is hard to imagine anyone who could better represent America as our ambassador in Jerusalem. This picture was taken as we celebrated Israel's National Day of Independence. After more than twenty years, we finally have a president who is ready to recognize Jerusalem as the eternal capital of the state of Israel, and the relations between the Jewish and American peoples have never been as strong as they are now. Let them always be so.

One of the rarely discussed pleasures of working in the White House is working with the US Secret Service. They're consummate professionals and wonderful people. (That includes you, Officer Mark—you know who you are!) Here I am with two female SS officers and my friends from the Counterterrorism Division of the NYPD, who were visiting the "swamp" and wanted to have a tour of the Trump White House.

My favorite painting in the entire White House.

More than just a meteorological phenomenon. After eight years in the wilderness, America is taking back her rightful place in the world.

One of Donald Trump's great virtues is his personal loyalty. If you demonstrate that you can be trusted and are loyal, he will always be loyal in return. I may not have a blue White House badge anymore, but that doesn't mean I don't hear from the president when he needs some advice or that my wife, Katie, and I don't get to visit on special occasions, the most important, of course, being Christmas.

Just a few days after leaving the White House to support the president from the outside, I was back in the thick of it. Here, I'm giving a press conference with members of the House, supporting our Kurdish friends in Iraq.

Before joining the White House, I spent most of my time working with fine Americans such as these soldiers from Fort Bragg or the Marines of Quantico. My dream was always to work with America's best and bravest, and the good Lord made it a reality after we moved to the United States.

If someone had told me just a few years ago, when I (legally!) immigrated to the US, that I would soon be standing next to the Resolute desk as strategist to the president, I would never have believed him. God bless America!
Courtesy of S. Craighead, Official White House Photograph

Sebastian Gorka: So we need a spine. Those of us that have a podium, those that are out there, those that wish to see the principles we believe in in terms of the Founding come back and be celebrated in this country, we have to call them out. We don't believe that you use legislation. I mean "hate speech"—give me a break. Either you're inciting violence or you're not. Either you're committing a crime or you're not. We don't need extra labels, and we don't need censorship. Call them out for what they are. We need people on the right who say, "You know what, he's a racist. That alt-right thing, that's just bigotry, that's just the KKK wrapped up in a new bow." It's up to us. The left's not going to do it. They're going to use it. They're going to use those people to silence the majority. Do I think that's happening? No, not enough by far. We have begun but there's a lot of work to do.

Dave: Does everything that's happening in Europe ... and there's definitely a distinction to be made between Eastern Europe and Western Europe. Eastern Europe is dealing with their existential crisis a little bit better perhaps because Western Europe's a little behind on the political correctness thing you're talking about. Does everything that's happening in Europe right now, does it all come down to immigration, do you think?

Sebastian Gorka: No. No, immigration was the blue touch paper on the firework. No, it's the death of representative democracy.

I watched this because I grew up in the UK under Margaret Thatcher. For me, Maggie, The Gipper, St. John Paul II, these were my heroes. And I remember riding to school on the bus in the morning in West London and the bus driver would be Jamaican. I'd be with my Indian or Pakistani school buddy. I'd be with this Polish guy next to me.

I mean it's a super heterogeneous part of London. As far as I was concerned, these were all Brits. The guy might have had the thickest Jamaican accent possible, my friend Martin's mum cooked the best Indian curries, but guess what, we were all British. That's gone.

When Tony Blair came in, when Clinton came in, this idea that the West is guilty and words like "British" are pejorative, you're a Gujarati, you're Welsh, you're whatever, that was the death of these countries. Why do you think I'm in America? I'm a proud American citizen now because they lost the plot. The things that the GIs fought for, that the Tommys fought for. I mean, safe spaces? Really? You had nineteen-year-olds that are being blown up over Berlin in bomber planes and you want a safe space? This is in a space of seventy years? I mean, what's going on in London right now. This is the land of Churchill!

Dave: I'm sure you saw this but just in the last couple weeks they said London's crime has surpassed New York City's for the first time in history. And then Sadiq Khan, who's the mayor, issued a statement saying you can't carry knives. I mean first off, people are walking around with Swiss army knives. A woman that might want to protect herself might want to carry a knife in her pocket. It seems like a mass mental disorder to me. It really does.

Sebastian Gorka: That's what happens. That is the natural progression when you deny objective truth. If everything is plastic, then you will get wrapped around your axel in absurdities. For a mayor of one of the most powerful cities in the world, a financial center to say, "No one should ever have a knife on them and nobody needs a knife." So every plumber, every tradesmen, every person working a fish market is suddenly out of a job? That's insane.

Dave: So what does Britain or Europe in a wider sense have to do to reverse the tide on some of this stuff?

Sebastian Gorka: Listen to people like Nigel Farrage, I don't know. I mean, look, this saying crops up in every nation: "Every country deserves the politicians they elect." Don't bitch and moan, get out there.

I see it where I live outside D.C., the conservative who is so fed up and constantly posting on Facebook. What have you done about it? Have you gone out with leaflets? Have you given more than five dollars to your local candidate? Have you given up and surrendered? I see this all the time. The people who say, "The greatest nation on earth" and then they say, "We're going purple, so many bureaucrats have moved in." What are you going do? Would you have said that in 1776? Would the Founding Fathers have said, "What are you going to do?" No.

Dave: Is this just a symptom of the success of the West—that we've just become so successful that we just sit there on Twitter and we don't do anything? It's all talk. It's not do.

Sebastian Gorka: It's more than that. It's deep. I went to the Jesuits. I studied philosophy under them. It was painful, but I won't regret a minute of it. Identity is a function of history and culture and values, and if you don't study Western civilization in your schools and your colleges this is what happens. If you don't understand why people have dignity, just that they do—oh, unless they're conservatives—this is where we arrive at.

And you know who's responsible for this. I don't blame the left, Dave. This is not the left's culpability. It's ours. It's conservatives.

The radicals, when they saw Paris on fire in 1968, they believed they could do the same to America, that we could have a left-wing revolution. This is what your Students for a Democratic Society believed, and when Bernardine Dohrn and Bill Ayers took over the SDS and tried to execute their Chicago "Days of Rage," what happened? Because Americans are not rabble-rousing leftists, it died. It was a damp squib. The Maoist revolution, the *Prairie Fire* manifesto[7] died instantly. So what did they decide? They'd read their Trotsky. They'd read their Lenin. They even knew what Hitler said: "Give me their children and I'll own their future."

These people actually became tenured professors in Chicago. They became high school teachers, and what did we do on the right? We let them. People who avowedly believe America is evil were allowed to influence our education system to the point to which they pretty much owned it with the exception of your Hillsdale College and Grove City College. They own the education system, and what was our response? Homeschooling. Great. I mean, I love the movement, but that's not going to save us, it's not enough. So it's going to be a hard slog. It's going to be twenty to thirty years of saying, "Guys, America means this and it's nothing to do with your skin color. It's nothing to do with your sexual preference, your social class, your gender. America is eternal values." And that's going to be a lot of work.

Dave: Okay. So I want to shift a little bit to foreign policy because I think that's sort of one of your main strengths.

Sebastian Gorka: My claim to fame is counter terrorism and stuff like this, but deep down I'm a strategy wonk. Grand strategy is my thing.

Dave: So we'll talk in the lens of strategy then. So, as we're taping this right now, like I was saying earlier, it's going to sit on the shelf for a couple days, so I don't want to get too lost in anything that happened today, but at the moment it's a little upside down in Syria. There might have been strikes already from when we were taping this. Hungary just had elections. In your Wikipedia, it says you worked for the guy that just won. Apparently, you never worked for him. What are your general thoughts on foreign policy strategy, and what is a sensible policy and is Trump applying that view?

Sebastian Gorka: First things first. The great irony of our nation is that we are the most powerful nation the world has ever seen, and until recently we have been the dumbest and most astrategic. I mean, we haven't thought or acted strategically since 1989, November the ninth, when the Berlin Wall fell.

Dave: How have we acted?

Sebastian Gorka: The '90s was just confused, "What-is-national-security about?" lurching for the snooze button. Who are the threats? Is it China? Is it weapons of mass destruction? Is it ethnic cleansing such as in Yugoslavia? It was just a mess, and then we had 2001, on 9/11, and we had the neocon disasters.

It's not an accident these guys are former Trotskyites, because they're so naïve at the way they look at the world. We're going to create democracy at the end of a gun barrel in a country with thirty-six languages that defeated Alexander the Great and the British Empire and the Soviets? You couldn't be stupider if you tried. So we've done some very foolish things because we haven't stuck to the basics.

Strategy, at the end of the day, is about one thing: It's about prioritization based on interests. You've got to say some things are more important than others and, guess what, some countries are more important than others. But in a postmodern secular world, you're not allowed to say that. All countries are equally important. Vanuatu is as important as Turkey. Wrong! It's not. I may love the people of Vanuatu, but no, it's not of geostrategic import to the country of America.

So, number one, we have to prioritize, and I think this administration does. I doff my cap to Nadia Schadlow, H. R. McMaster's deputy. She held the pen in the meetings that I was in on new *National Security Strategy*[8] of America, and I tell you, Dave, it is the first document in thirty years that deserves the name "National Security Strategy." Every administration has them. This is the first one that says, this is what we stand for, these are our friends, these are our enemies, and this is what we're going to prioritize. Prior to that it was laundry lists—we're going to have two large wars at once, we're going to save the whales. You have to prioritize.

Finally, this administration is about "America first." We are not isolationists, nor are we interventionists. This really annoys me. If you're a conservative, for twenty years, you were given two choices: Button A: Invade other people's countries and occupy them. Button B: Close the curtains on the Pacific and the Atlantic and say, "We don't care about anybody else." Well, for the most powerful nation in the world there is a large palette of options between the two! It's about being smart and it's about our interests.

To summarize the president's approach, this isn't official, but I like it. We have numerous former generals and active generals from the Marine Corps at the highest levels of the administration, the chairman of Joint Chiefs, the chief of staff, the secretary of defense, and the interesting thing is they all come from the same Marine Corps Division—not just the Marine Corps, but the same division.

That division has a motto: "No better Friend. No worse Enemy." That's "America first."

Dave: So when you see someone like John Bolton being now part of the cabinet, and if you were to look, not that you can get truth out of Twitter, but the day it was happening, everybody was saying that this is going to start World War III and just the general hysterics. Now John Bolton is definitely, I suspect, more of a neocon than you would be comfortable with ...

Sebastian Gorka: I don't think it's fair to call him a neocon. I don't think he's ideologically driven. If you watch the videos recorded of his speeches twenty years ago, he was sounding very much like Trump. "We're Americans and we have interests. If you want to work with us, fine. If you don't, there's a problem." I think it's very telling that within forty minutes of the president's tweet about John coming on board, Bolton gave an interview on Fox, and they asked him about what are you going to be like as a national security advisor, and he gave a very interesting answer. He quoted Dean Acheson, the doyen of foreign policy in America. I don't know if this is a true story, but John said, "Dean Acheson was once asked, 'How do you have such a good relationship with the president you serve?' and Dean Acheson said, 'Well it's very easy. We may disagree on policy issues, but at the end of the day, I never forget who was elected president, and it wasn't me.'" That's a John Bolton 2.0. He understands that, unlike his predecessor H. R. McMaster, he's not there to lecture the president and foist his version of what you should do onto the commander in chief but to be an honest broker and provide a palette of options because the person who was elected president gets to decide. So I'm very excited about John, and I'm as excited about Mike Pompeo coming from the

CIA to the State Department. We are in very good hands, Dave.

Dave: So how do you make sure, if it's between the pure isolationists and the neocons or something like the nation-builders that not everything that you do outside of our borders becomes something much bigger. I mean, look, we're still at war in Afghanistan. I don't think anyone knows why. Can you tell me why we're at war in Afghanistan? Can anyone tell us at this point?

Sebastian Gorka: I'll tell you why we went to Afghanistan in October of '01, and it still is the only reason we should be there today. Nothing's changed.

The idea that girls can go to school—I love it, I get it. And that people can listen to music freely and the Taliban won't execute you. My parents lived under communism. My father suffered under fascism. He protected his Jewish classmates during the occupation of Budapest. I don't like those kinds of systems, but there was only one reason we were there: to make sure that that land-mass would not be used to execute mass casualty attacks in Manhattan, in Washington, or in a field in Pennsylvania. End of story.

It's not about building a ring road around Kabul that not even the Soviets could finish. It's not about building hospitals. I'm sorry, you never make the ideal the enemy of the good. What the president does is he looks at things as questions of possibility. You can't be a massively successful realtor in the toughest market in the world, New York real estate, if you have a filter that distorts reality. Either this square footage is worth x or it's not worth x according to the market, and that's how he approaches these issues. So Afghanistan's only important to make sure that bad guys don't use it again to kill Americans in America.

Dave: So you would say, or at least if you had to gues-timate basically what he believes, you would say that he believes that still keeping us there at the moment is still accomplishing …

Sebastian Gorka: Oh yeah, I don't have the guestimate. I can tell you that.

Dave: So you believe that as well, because it seems unclear to me …

Sebastian Gorka: He will never, this seventy-one-year-old man who is now the most powerful man in the world, will never, ever buy into a nation-building scenario any-where outside of the United States. It's not happening for the next seven years. And that idea that you have some of my followers on Twitter tearing their hair out that "Bolton's going to have us invade Syria." Guys, get a grip on reality and stop talking about "crisis actors" and similar tin-foil-hat garbage. It's not going to happen while the president is the president.

Dave: Well I tweeted something to that effect the day of the Bolton thing because it also reminds me that to understand basic deterrence, that you have to bring in people that, you know, talk a big game so that …

Sebastian Gorka: North Korea! Hello! The man who was "going to take us to war," what did he do? I think the success in North Korea today has in large part been thanks to his tweets, because that's how you deal with dictators. You make fun of them. They hate that and then you ridi-cule them. And then what? You scare them. Oh, and lo and behold, they want to negotiate for the first time in sixty-five years. Well, isn't that interesting?

Dave: Do you think there's any chance [Kim] would give up his nukes?

Sebastian Gorka: About three percent.

Dave: Because at that point what leverage does he have left, right? But you still think it's worth having the talks to figure out what we can do.

Sebastian Gorka: Absolutely, because what's happened for the last twenty-five years? Escalation, escalation, escalation. I mean we have given in to nuclear blackmail since Bill Clinton. So at the end of the day, we have to remember that 1953 was not a peace treaty. 1953 in Korea was a ceasefire and an armistice. That is actually a war that has simply been frozen for sixty-five years. It would be nice to have a little bit of a peace treaty or something!

Dave: How much of what's happening in the world right now—you must be thrilled I assume with everything going on at the UN. Nikki Haley has basically walked in there, and she strikes me, I almost wonder did Trump really know what he was getting with her fully? Do you know her at all? Where do you think that comes from?

Sebastian Gorka: She found herself. She found herself, and more power to her.

Dave: What usefulness do you see in the UN at this point? Truly it is the most corrupt, backwards ...

Sebastian Gorka: Look, the idea was a good idea in 1945 in San Francisco. Let's have an organization that stops us from killing sixty million people again, but when you lock in dictatorships like China and Russia on the Security Council, with veto power, and then you create this empire of UN organizations .... I mean has there been a year in the last twenty years that we haven't seen a UN scandal, whether it's money-for-oil, whether it's UN troops raping children in Africa? Have we seen one year without a UN scandal? I don't think so. So try and reform, and if you can't question the validity of what it does. I'm not talking about the children's rights organizations and food security. I'm talking about its main mission, which was stability and safety. It's failed abysmally.

Dave: What do you make of the endless obsession with Israel? That something like forty-seven of the last fifty-one resolutions are against Israel and usually voted on by countries ...

Sebastian Gorka: I'm sorry, but that alone is a reason to dissolve the UN. What a lack of a moral compass. What an utter bankruptcy of their morality that there are nations in the world that actually still have slavery going on. Slavery! Where basic human rights for individuals are not guaranteed based upon sex, based upon lifestyle choices, and you're going to lambast Israel, the only real democracy in the Middle East? Yes, I think you nailed it. That in itself is reason to question the future of the UN.

Dave: So is the US sort of in an odd position where if we don't do anything nothing can get done, and that then puts us endlessly in these quagmires, or at least in these positions where we can either watch the world burn or get involved in things where we may end up adding to the burning in the first place?

Like, for example, with Russia going into Crimea. You know, [the Crimeans] gave up their weapons and they said, "Okay, NATO is going to take care of us," but what that really means is the United States is going to take care of you, and I'm not saying we should have gone in and done anything there, but that we're in this endless situation now where it is either us—there is no international fighting force, really—right?

Sebastian Gorka: But again you have to be super careful not to get caught in a binary dichotomy. You can absolutely say a world without American leadership is a more dangerous world, because it was for the last eight years. We had a government that actually said "We're going to lead from behind," which is an oxymoron. You cannot lead from behind. "We're going to have strategic patience," which means we do nothing and allow others to act. What happened? You name it. From China building fake military bases on fake islands to ISIS to Russia invading Ukraine. It was just a disaster.

Dave: Egypt, we backed the guy, then we backed the other guys, then we backed the other guys!

Sebastian Gorka: To say that a world without American leadership is more dangerous is true, but that doesn't mean that we have to fix everybody's problem, and that's where smart strategy comes in.

We have a moral duty to espouse certain values, but that doesn't mean we are responsible for all human beings, because the American Revolution says the opposite. Each nation is responsible. Their citizens are responsible. If you don't like your system, do something about it. We did against the most powerful empire in the world. So again, it's about finding that happy medium in the middle and being smart about it and, again, without being callous, just being realistic. There are atrocities everywhere from Rwanda to Yugoslavia, but are American taxpayers going to pay for fixing all of them? Are we responsible? Are they responsible for what's happening in their country? Sure. Are there times when we could perhaps help them? Uh-huh, but it's a balance.

Dave: So let's shift back to your book *Defeating Jihad*.

It seems to me that the main sort of narrative on this out there is not that we can defeat it but we should live with it, which is don't carry knives in London, and we're going to put up more barricades so that trucks can't be driven into buildings or into shopping centers or just down the street and killing people. That we can't really defeat this ideology; we just have to manage it. I suspect that you do not agree with that premise.

Sebastian Gorka: No, because we've defeated ideologies before.

Look, there are idiots who run around with swastika armbands today. So Nazism hasn't disappeared, but we have made it so anathema that if you walk down the street with a Nazi flag, you will be rejected by society instantly. The same thing with the KKK. Sadly, not with Che Guevara, or the hammer and sickle, but there are ways to defeat ideologies or to put them in a box where they're laughable and everybody shuns them. We have to do the same thing with jihadism. This is my argument. This is the conclusion of the book. We have to be as effective at delegitimizing the message of jihad. Very simply put, killing jihadis is great, but at the end of the day, body bags as a metric, that's not a good metric. It didn't work in Vietnam, and it doesn't work today, because if you've got a recruiting pool that's massive, they'll just recruit more jihadis.

So what's your victory condition? Your victory condition is when the lifestyle of jihad is no longer sexy from Brussels to San Bernardino. How do you do that? You make a laughing stock, you discredit that value system. Not us. I mean, a white-skinned Catholic isn't going to do it, but we help President Sisi. We help King Abdullah of Jordan. We help MBS [Mohammad bin Salman] in Saudi Arabia. MBS is saying historic things, massive things about Israel in just the last few weeks. That's how we win, because sooner or later enough people say, "Nah, those guys are losers." That's how we win, but you only do that if you get to talk about it truthfully. You've got to be able to talk about the Koran, what jihad means, the history of the religion, because if you can't talk about it honestly, you're never going to treat it accurately.

Dave: We're not very good at that, though.

Sebastian Gorka: Thanks to political correctness. Imagine if you're a doctor, and you've got a patient that comes in with third-stage lymphoma, but your hospital administrator, because it's a scary word, has banned the use of the word "cancer." It's just not allowed. And then you have to tell the patient what? "Well you've got the flu, you're dehydrated. Go home, drink water, and take some aspirin." What happens to your patient? They die. It's the same thing. If you can't diagnose a geostrategic issue accurately, however much money you throw at it, you will not solve the problem.

Dave: So are you concerned at all that, even if it is just because of the way the media frames things, that perhaps Trump is not the right person to lead the fight against this, that for whatever he's going to say about jihad or radical Islamic terrorism or the rest, that even if he said everything the exact way that you wanted it to be said, cleanly and clearly and correctly defined and all of that, that he may not be the right messenger for this just because of the filter it would have to get through to reality?

Sebastian Gorka: He's not the right messenger domestically because of what political correctness has wrought in this country, but he's absolutely the right messenger internationally. Watch the video of his Riyadh speech.[9] Don't watch him. Watch the fifty-three Muslim and Arab heads of state and their body language, because, man, did he [tell it to them straight]: "Guys, you've got a problem in your mosques, in your society, the extremists, etc. you've got to deal with it!" It was tough.

You'd think they'd be all negative and arms crossed. But they were beaming. Sisi, Abdullah were going, "Well finally, a guy who understands our problem and is giving us tough love." So yes, he is absolutely the right guy to fix this internationally, which is where it needs to be fixed. Domestically, no, the political correctness thing is going to get in the way and the media insanity.

Dave: Do you think he has more support from foreign heads of state than we'll ever have a sense of? I mean, even at the G8 there was a feeling of actually these guys kind of liked him.

Sebastian Gorka: I can tell you, yes. I told people before the inauguration, you have no idea, even if you voted for him, you have no idea how successful he will be internationally because he's a straight shooter and because he's an alpha dog, and in a lot of places outside of Berkeley they like that, because they know what you're talking about. They don't have to walk on egg shells. They understand your direction. So yes, internationally, our prestige as a nation has skyrocketed outside the European Union, and maybe certain Central European countries exempted, but yes, absolutely.

Dave: So I know we could do a whole other show on this, but very quickly just on Russia and "collusion," as someone that has been around the administration, you've mentioned some of these people already, like Flynn. What can you tell me about that? And is there anything that people should be worried about, or do you think that this will all just point back to the Democrats? Which every time it seems to point to Trump, you go a little bit further, and it's like, "Oh, that was actually the Democrats."

Sebastian Gorka: My good friend has the best morning show in D.C., Chris Plante; he is the radio host. It's actually nationally syndicated now, and I have to credit him with this. He says it's like the last scene from *The*

Hunt for Red October, when the bad captain, Tupolev, launches the torpedo against Sean Connery on the *Red October*, and he takes the fuses off and then what happens? His XO says, "You idiot. You've killed us." The thing comes back and sinks them. This is the most hilarious boomerang in history.

I'll tell you what the president told me in the Oval Office, just the two of us. He was very frustrated one day. I think maybe Jared had just testified or given his speech, his little press conference. He said, "They will not find anything because there is nothing." You know what? I take that to the bank. There is no Russian collusion. How could there be after the last fifteen months? From arming the Ukrainians, to the XL Pipeline, to Anwar [in Alaska], to finally after thirty years the first president to ever get NATO to finally stump up the two percent of GDP that they promised they'd spend on defense, to our own military expenditure increases, every significant policy decision this president has taken with regards to Russia has been bad for that former KGB colonel [Putin]. So the idea that we're colluding? You'd have to be on drugs or so ideologically blind to believe that.

Dave: Well then, what do we do with this "Deep State"? What do we do with this thing? I mean, look, we have this ongoing investigation, the Mueller investigation, what seems odd to me is that I don't know what the actual … I don't know that they ever laid out what their mission is other than to find something.

Sebastian Gorka: What was the crime? "Collusion" is not a crime. Collusion to conspire in a crime, okay, but what's the crime? Because if it's Russia misrepresenting itself or perverting the truth on Facebook, well then Zuckerburg should be charged. Well, then Anderson Cooper should be in the dock. What are the charges that have been brought? Outrageously ridiculous ones: lying to federal investigators. You would probably be able to be caught in a perjury trap today. Because not everybody remembers what they did and how they did it. Perjury traps about what you said to somebody, irrespective of Russia. That's not Donald Trump's problem. Wire fraud, eight years ago, when Manafort worked for the Ukrainian president? What's that got to do with Russian collusion? Nothing.

My worry is that Mueller is not a good actor. If you look at whom he's hired, it's clear that there's massive bias, and this report he's writing for Congress is simply going to be a political weapon in the elections. That's not how justice is served. That's not rule of law. That's a law enforcement official getting involved in politics.

Dave: So that's what I'm concerned about also. Whether you think something happened or didn't happen, what I'm more concerned about is that we're entering this new phase where, whether it's Trump that's president or it's a Democrat that's president or a different Republican or whatever, that we're just going to endlessly also have this layer that all it does is investigate itself, waste money, constantly keep us all in this state where we never know what's real. Because if you listen to half of the pundits on television, their implication is that Russia has installed our president. In which case, that's probably the single biggest act of war in the history of the world, and what are you actually saying? Do you take Trump out? And then do you take out Pence? And now should Paul ... I mean if you take it to its logical conclusion ... do we have Paul Ryan as president then? I mean, where are we really taking this? And what I'm worried about is that we're just going to be in this constant state where, yes, we'll have a Democrat and then a Republican

or whatever, but we'll really be caught in just all government can do is investigate itself really more than anything
else.

Sebastian Gorka: I see myself as an optimist, but you're
giving me a real challenge with that last one. So for months
and months and months, I refused to use the phrase "Deep
State." I really thought that was a tinfoil-hatty kind of
thing.

Dave: For the record, I don't even know that I've ever
said it once on this show. It sort of pops up in ancillary
ways.

Sebastian Gorka: But, Dave, I use it now because I've
seen it.

I've seen it inside the administration. When you go
to enough National Security Council meetings that are
classified, that is the pinnacle of policy-making in America outside of the Oval Office. I mean this is where policy is made. Everybody in the room is from the NSC.
Then you've got the outstations on secure video telecon-
ference from the Defense Intelligence Agency, the chairman of the Joint Chiefs, the CIA, State, you name it, and
you sit there as a newly appointed political, and you
listen for two hours on a big issue—ISIS, Russia, whatever it is—and not one participant mentions the name
of the president or what he said yesterday in Warsaw, or
what his objective is given that specific issue. And you
see this happen again and again and again, and you're
the guy at the end of the conversation with a funny
accent who says, "Excuse me, ladies and gentlemen, you
do know what the president said about *x* yesterday. Can
we actually do that?"

The Deep State is real. When you've got GS-15s and
SESs [Senior Executive Service] saying, "I've been here for

twenty years. This guy's going to be here for four. I know better." That's bad for democracy.

Dave: So to be clear. You don't think it's some kind of massive underground conspiracy. You think it's just the apparatus. It's just the old Washington apparatus.

Sebastian Gorka: You know these people who think Obama is sitting in a cave somewhere with a joystick? No. He's lazy. He'd never be a mastermind. It's not SPECTRE and he's not Blofeld.

No, but there's a culture in government that's antithetical to, and undermining, the president on a daily basis. But there is concerted effort in the media. Oh my gosh! I mean Ben Rhodes brags about it. When he says, "My buddies the left-wing journalists are morons, and they're my echo chamber." He built this machine that was this incestuous connection between people in the West Wing, people in the think-tank community, and their buddies in the media. Just look at the attack pieces on anybody, me, or whatever. It's very interesting. Somebody should do a case study in journalism school. One attack piece will drop at seven am. By two o'clock in the afternoon, thirty have been written, which were simply cut and paste, but if you don't know that, it looks that "Oh my gosh, Gorka's a fascist." But it's one guy's article that was written because Ben Rhodes told him to write it that comes and gets multiplied.

On the right, how do we react? "Well, I got my op-ed into *National Review* this month." There's a gulf in terms of managing narrative. The left built a whole ecosystem, and we're still in the 1980s, you know. We say, "Oh, we'll take out a full-page ad in the *Washington Times*." [It's just not enough].

Dave: I think most people, because of the way social media works, they immediately go to the full-on conspiracy of Obama with a joystick or just some other version of the globalist thing, whereas what you just described is more realistic to me—that there's an apparatus there that is still connected to the media. We can discuss that in a sensible way.

Sebastian Gorka: With one addition, and I appreciate this, being in the crosshairs for so long. They have an advantage because our side is predicated on what, Dave? On the individual, on manifest destiny, rugged individualism. We believe in the individual. The left by definition is a collective entity. There are elements of the Borg in the left. It is truly a collective mob mentality. When one guy goes after Gorka or Bannon or whomever, after the president, there's a massive, collective pile-on. It's not a conspiracy, but they're all singing from the same hymnal. They don't need direction, but they say, "Oh yeah, let's go after him." Which puts us on the right at a disadvantage.

Dave: So this is just sort of an emergent group thing.

Sebastian Gorka: It's a cultural thing.

Dave: Wow, we're going to do this again.

Sebastian Gorka: I hope so. This was so much fun!

Dave: It's been an absolute pleasure. For more on Dr. Gorka—you know you really should be a Star Wars character!—for more on Sebastian, follow him on Twitter, it's @SebGorka.

From West London to the West Wing

*T*he last two years have been quite a ride.

Why We Fight was written before I moved into the White House, but I feel I owe you, dear reader, a few words on how I became strategist to the president of the United States.

If anyone had said to me twenty years ago, or ten or five years ago, that this British-born immigrant to the United States would be walking around the West Wing of the White House as a deputy to the president, I would have thought him clinically insane—but there it was. A reality TV star who had never held public office became our commander in chief, and a legal immigrant with a funny accent became one of his political appointees. Only in America.

Truth be told, I always loved America. I may have been born and raised in West London to refugees from communist Hungary, but something about the States pulled me like a magnet. From my childhood, watching reruns of TV classics such as *Kojak*, *Starsky and Hutch*, and *The Streets of San Francisco* on British TV, to my student days at the University of London, buying a beat up '76 Chevy Camaro, something about the brash, no-excuses attitude of Americans simply resonated with me.

My parents were Hungarian, and my formative years were shaped by their experiences and the stories they told me about life in war-torn Budapest and then under the oppression of communist dictatorship. But during the Cold War years, this family history strengthened my attachment to all things American. It was clear to me that it would take US leadership and might to win that conflict against the new totalitarians, just as it had against the Nazis and fascists before.

When the Berlin Wall fell and the West won that ideological war, it was natural for me to take that heritage and try to live it. So, at the ripe age of twenty-three, I moved to the land of my forefathers, the newly free Hungarian Republic. My idealistic goal was to help the country my parents had fled rebuild itself as a functioning Western nation, to assist where possible in its re-entry into the community of Western nations. With the English, French, and German languages under my belt, the rudimentary Hungarian I had learnt at home, and the experience of a stint in the British Army reserves, I got a job in the Ministry of Defense (MoD) of the first post-communist government of Hungary.

Those five years in the MoD deserve a book themselves. For a young man who had grown up in Margaret Thatcher's Britain, going to live and work in a nation suppressed by forty years of communism was akin to beaming down from the Starship Enterprise onto some unknown planet—and without Spock to assist me. But that's another story. During those years, I met my muse and my eternal partner, Katie, at an international conference on ethnic conflict held in Romania, of all places. She had flown in from her think tank job in New York, and I from the MoD in Budapest.

It was love at first sight for both of us, and a year and half later, we were married. Soon children came, and then we went into business together, establishing the first independent think tank in Hungary dealing with national security issues and the challenges nations face when moving from dictatorship to democracy. God was good to us, as I was awarded back-to-back fellowships, first as a researcher at the NATO Defense College in Rome and then at Harvard's Kennedy School of Government. After the fellowships, we returned to Hungary, at which point history interrupted.

I will remember forever what I was doing when the first plane hit the Twin Towers. I was sitting in a Budapest cafe preparing my notes for a college class I was to teach the next day when my phone rang. Although a private citizen at this point, I was still plugged into the national security world and was helping with a visit by members of the US intelligence community to the new Secret Services minster of the conservative Hungarian administration. The minster's chief of staff was on the line, and he said, "Well I guess tomorrow's meeting is off now." When I asked what happened, he said to switch on a television.

My wife and I did not have cable because we had children and figured it was best not to. We still don't, even though our children are grown now. It was a good decision. I rushed to the home of dear friends, an American diplomat and his wife who had cable in their apartment. My wife was already there, and along with most of the world, we watched the impact of the second plane and all the subsequent horrors of that Tuesday.

September 11, 2001 would change history, and it would change our lives. We watched Hungarian public television with consternation. As live CNN footage ran in the background, an anchorman who knew English translated the US coverage. Then my wife said something that would prove consequential: "You're probably the only person in Hungary who speaks Hungarian and English and could speak meaningfully about this attack." Indeed, I had served in a reserve military intelligence unit in the British Army and had been studying terrorism for a decade by that time, working on the issue at

RAND and writing on it regularly for the British military publishing house, Janes. "Call up the TV station!" she said. I responded that life doesn't work that way. I was wrong.

Our friends handed me the phonebook (remember that?), and at Katie's insistence, I called the main number for the national broadcaster and asked for the duty editor. I told him who I was and my qualifications, and he asked me, "How fast can you get to the studio?" I said, "Forty minutes." It wasn't far away, but I was dressed casually and needed to go home to put on a suit. He replied, "If you're here in thirty, we're putting you on." I sped home, made myself presentable, rushed to the beautiful headquarters of Hungarian TV, and spent the next six hours on live television, never before having been in front of a camera.

That's how I became a household name in the land of my parents, as I spent the weeks and months after the 9/11 attacks appearing all over the media and analyzing what would become President's Bush's Global War on Terror. And because of that exposure, I was recognized by a retired Marine Corps legend who had his own post-9/11 mission.

Colonel Andrew Nichols Pratt, or Nick, had served with distinction with the marines as well as the CIA as a paramilitary working in Afghanistan against the Soviets in the 1980s. After retiring from active duty, he stayed with the Defense Department as a professor at the George C. Marshall Center in Garmisch-Partenkirchen, a Pentagon facility at the foot of the Alps in Bavaria. With his typical pragmatism, and long before anyone else came up with the catchy phrase, "It takes a network to defeat a network," Nick realized that al-Qaeda was a globally diffused organization that would take a global partnership of new allies to win the war against global jihadism.

Thanks to that vision and the funding Nick acquired from the Office of the Assistant Secretary of Defense for Special Operations and Low-Intensity Conflict, Garmisch became the home to the Program on Terrorism and Security Studies, a six-week intensive course on the evolution of terrorism and how to defeat groups like al-Qaeda, which was open to senior counterterrorism professionals from around the world. Nick asked me to become a founding "plank holder" member of his faculty.

It was an incredible and glorious four years working with colonels and one-star generals from all over the planet—from Pakistan to Poland, from Trinidad and Tobago to Thailand—and I learnt a great deal from the intrepid men who were often already fighting jihadis on their own soil. But by 2008, I had a hankering.

Our classes always included a few American students, mostly Special Forces types, but also members of the Intelligence Community and the FBI. After a while, I found myself connecting to these brave souls and wanting to serve their broader community more specifically. Working for Nick had opened doors and seriously expanded my Rolodex, so in the spring of that year, I applied to be a professor to three American military institutions: West Point, the Virginia Military Institute, and the Defense Department's highest educational institution, the National Defense University (NDU) in Washington, D.C. I visited all three locations and was duly impressed, but it was NDU, located on beautiful Fort McNair, one of our oldest bases, that offered me a position first. After fifteen years in Hungary with two small children, Katie and I upped sticks completely: I became a legal immigrant, fifty-two years after my parents had done the same.

That was a decade ago. Our children have grown up in America, and both Katie and I have made new careers for ourselves. Until 2016, mine revolved almost exclusively around the military, law enforcement, and intelligence. I spent almost six years at NDU, ending up as associate dean for congressional affairs and relations to the Special Forces community. At the same time, I taught with increasing frequency for the Joint Special Operations University at US Special Operations Command in Florida and for the John F. Kennedy Special Warfare Center and School in Fort Bragg, home to the Green Berets. After a few years, Katie and I established our own company to provide specialized education and analysis to the US government, specifically on the evolution of al-Qaeda and new groups like ISIS. Our company became the exclusive external provider of congressionally-mandated counterterrorism training to the FBI, and we ran a multi-year project on irregular warfare for US Army Special Operations Command. Then, I received a call from Trump Tower. Some of the details of this story you will find out in my interview about with Dave Rubin. But not all of them!

It was the summer of 2015, and I was no longer in government service. In addition to running our company, I held a privately-endowed teaching position at the Marine Corps University, Quantico, the corps' own version of NDU. As the occupant of the Major General Matthew C. Horner Chair of Military Theory, I was teaching at the various schools on the Quantico complex, including the Command and Staff College—which Colonel Pratt had once commanded—the War College, and the Enlisted and Captains schools. It was a career pinnacle. But then, Corey Lewandowski called my cell phone and said that "candidate Trump" would like to meet me.

The future president was preparing for a big Republican debate on national security, and he wanted someone to advise him on key issues, such as defeating ISIS. Would I come to Trump Tower to meet him? Of course, I would.

I flew to New York, and the three of us met in Donald Trump's office. In the midst of a wide-range discussion about all kinds of issues, Mr. Trump stopped in the middle of a sentence, turned to Corey, and said, "I like this guy! Let's hire him!" Pure Trump. And that's how I became a consultant to the future president of the United States. Over the next few months, I would also get to know General Mike Flynn, and before the election, I was made a member of the official National Security Council Transition Team. And then, we won.

I continued to work for Mike Flynn until just before the inauguration. Less than a week before I was to begin working in the White

House on counterterrorism for the National Security Council under General Flynn, Steve Bannon intervened.

I had helped Steve when I was working with the marines in Quantico by serving as his national security editor at Breitbart, a "quality control" function, making sure that the articles on that vertical were as strong as they could be. The man who had come in and brought Trump from sixteen points behind Hillary to victory, Steve was now coming into the West Wing to serve as chief strategist to the president. And he wanted me working for him as strategist to the president. That is how, at eight o'clock in the morning on Saturday, January 21, 2017, I found myself walking around the White House, not as a tourist, but as a politically commissioned officer of the forty-fifth president.

This journey is a typically American one, and I never forget it. Every day as I walked in and out of the West Wing, as I attended NSC meetings or represented the president's policies on national television. I would constantly pinch myself as a reminder that I am an immigrant and this truly is the greatest nation on God's Earth.

My next book will deal in detail with my time in the White House, who President Trump really is (no Fake News), and how he has always been so incredibly successful. With *Why We Fight*, I have tried to show you why we are unique as a nation, how we defeat those who wish to harm us, and to share with you the incredible stories of some truly heroic Americans.

Until next time, have faith, never give up, and be a part of Making America Great Again. Godspeed.

Want to Know More about How to Always Win?

What I Read, Watch, and Listen To

I live and breathe national security. I love strategy. I am a political junkie and spend too much time on "social" media. At least according to my wife.

We live in an age of information overload. I remember a time when, if you wanted to look up a fact or learn about something new, you had to go to a library or at least leaf through an encyclopedia. Not anymore.

Today, with a browser and a few apps, you have access to more information than any traditional library could hold. And that is a good thing, but doesn't mean we are all smarter and have all the answers.

The internet is awash with nonsense, misinformation, insane conspiracy theories, and stories that are ideologically slanted or just plain wrong. This problem is greatly exacerbated by two other facts of life here at the beginning of the third millennium.

First, the so-called academic and intellectual "elite" is nothing of the sort. Just look at the last few years. For example, the policy "elite" thought it would be smart to invade Afghanistan and Iraq, in the belief that they could be turned into functioning democracies. And as for academia, many, maybe even most, of the professors teaching our youth believe there are more than fifty "genders" and that socialism is a good thing.

Second, no one reads anymore. Not books, anyway. Just look at the most prevalent social media platforms. The most powerful medium, Twitter, limits you to 280 characters. Not words, but characters. The famously concise Gettysburg Address has 270 words—more than nine hundred characters. Even those who have mastered the video monster that is YouTube stress that shorter is better. A three-minute video is great, they say. And you're crazy if you think viewers will pay attention for thirty or forty minutes.

As a result, sitting down for hours at a time to read a physical book is, for millions, an unknown experience. Disconnecting from Facebook, Twitter, email, and your phone for long enough to read one chapter of a book can seem like a challenge today, but it shouldn't. Real knowledge doesn't come in a tweet, a video of cute animals, or even a topical podcast on a singular subject. It comes from immersing yourself in a subject again and again over a prolonged period. Trust me.

I have been teaching for more than twenty years in institutions ranging from the Special Warfare Center and School in Fort Bragg to Georgetown University. I would never have dared stand up in front of a room of Green Berets or graduate students if I had tried to master my subject using only the internet. Knowledge—real knowledge—requires an investment of time and the reading of actual books with physical pages. Would you trust yourself to a surgeon whose training was limited to watching videos of how to do an appendectomy? Right.

So, if you liked this book, then my first bit of advice is this: read another one. And then another, and another. Or do what I do, and have half a dozen going at once!

Nevertheless, I am not a neo-Luddite who rejects all modern media. The tools on your Android or iPhone can be incredibly powerful. And to be honest, when you find a good podcast by a knowledgeable host who has read some books, it can be addictive. The real challenge is to separate the wheat from the chaff, to be able to identify rapidly what is worth reading—because few books are—and who is worth watching or listening to. And in that endeavor, I would like to be your humble guide, at least when it comes to the subjects and issues we have touched upon in *Why We Fight*.

What follows is a list of people and platforms I trust and respect for those who want to know more. In no way is this an exhaustive list. For that, you will have to check out one of my syllabi and take one of my graduate courses (if I ever get back to my passion of graduate school teaching). In the meantime, treat this as "phase two" of your journey to wisdom in all things national security and all matters strategic and political. Have fun.

GENERAL NEWSY STUFF

How do you keep up to date on all that's going on out there, especially in the Age of Trump, when the president moves as fast as he does and when the majority of "mainstream" media coverage really is #FakeNews?

Personally, I get much of my daily news from the radio. I love to drive, and radio allows me to absorb the latest information as I get from one place to another. Thirty years ago, Rush Limbaugh changed talk radio forever, and now conservative news analysis is by far the most influential radio there is. You can trust the shows that come out of the Salem Radio Network, which includes such luminaries as Dennis Prager, Larry Elder, Mike Gallagher, and Eric Metaxas. "The Great

One," Mark Levin, and my friend and colleague, Sean Hannity, are right up there with Rush with their daily shows, as are my good friends Chris Plante, Lars Larson, and Larry O'Connor, and the master of the long-form interview, John Batchelor. Listening regularly to these programs will give you what you need to know about events of the day with a sound, conservative, no-nonsense analysis.

When it comes to the goggle-box (TV) and internet video or podcasts—unless you want to raise your blood pressure by watching CNN and the rest of the "Fake News Industrial Complex" (a phrase invented by my former White House colleague Andy Surabian), stick to shows on Fox News. Other challengers on the right include One America News Network and Newsmax, but both have a ways to go in terms of range and capacity. The Sinclair Broadcast Group of regional, non-cable stations is also giving the Left a healthy run for its money.

When it comes to my friends at Fox, Sean Hannity is the leader of the pack with perennially the most popular cable news show in America. Sean's herculean feat of hosting his television show five days a week while running a three-hour daily radio show is testimony to his dedication and sense of mission. But don't miss out on the rest of the winning Fox team, including the excellent morning crew on Fox and Friends, Tucker Carlson, and the super shows on the Fox Business Network, led by the unstoppable Lou Dobbs, Stuart Varney, Trish Reagan, Maria Bartiromo, Charles Payne, Elizabeth MacDonald, and the rest of the FBN team. And yes, I can confirm that more than one of these shows is regular viewing for a certain current resident of the White House, so you are in good company!

For the younger, more internet-based freedom-lovers out there, there are of course the news sites that compete with the mostly left-wing legacy media. You can trust sites like the Daily Caller, the Federalist, Real Clear Politics, PJ Media, and Breitbart—yes, I said it!

For those who still need to get their fingers covered in print ink, stick to the *Washington Times* and *New York Post*—you cannot beat the latter for its cover pages! For longer analyses, I recommend the *American Thinker* and *City Journal*. And if you want the crème de la crème of conservative intellectual nourishment, do yourself a favor and subscribe to the *Claremont Review of Books* and Hillsdale College's *Imprimis*.

Among the growing sea of blogs and podcasts, my personal favorites are Andrew Klavan, the brave and funny Steven Crowder, Dan Bongino, the fiery Michelle Malkin, Rusty Humphries, and of course, Mark Levin. I am also an addict of YouTube video lectures. You will always learn something from investing an hour into watching a lecture or debate with the likes of true thinkers such as Niall Ferguson or Victor Davis Hanson. Also see the YouTube lectures provided by the Westminster Institute and the Institute of World Politics, which represent a collection of graduate-level education for free.

BECOMING A REAL EXPERT

As I am sure you have gathered, I love strategy. Reading and thinking big things about national security really is my "bag." If you want to navigate your way through all the garbage that is out there and become conversant in the eternal truths of statecraft and international affairs, ignore the "elite" publications like *Foreign Affairs* and *Foreign Policy* in addition to the same old same old boilerplate pumped out by the pseudo-experts at places like the Council on Foreign Relations, CSIS, Carnegie, CNAS, and Brookings, who have done so much damage to our nation in recent decades. Even the RAND Corporation, where I cut my policy teeth in the late nineties, is a shadow of its former illustrious self. Today, it produces one anodyne, boring, and irrelevant report after another, funded most often by your taxpayer dollars and deliberately safe so as not to jeopardize the next juicy government contract.

Instead, I suggest you stick to the basics and educate yourself.

Read the ever-shrinking number of sound and serious periodicals such as *Orbis*, *Military Review*, and the US Army's *Parameters*. Stick to reading the original works of the greats, such as Clausewitz and Sun Tzu, and the works of the few people alive today who have truly earned the right to be called "strategists." That list includes Colin Gray, a former adviser to President Reagan, Martin van Creveld of Israel, the quintessentially iconoclastic Ed Luttwak, the splendid Victor Davis Hanson, Carnes Lord, Niall Ferguson, and Angelo Codevilla.

When it comes to going deeper on the threats and the stories I have written about in *Why We Fight*, here is some further reading:

On our first war with the jihadis, more about Stephen Decatur, and what followed under the Barbary Wars, refer to Alexander Mackenzie's *Life of Stephen Decatur: A Commodore in the Navy of the United States*; Spencer Tucker's *Stephen Decatur: A Life Most Bold and Daring*; and Gardner Weld Allen's *Our Navy and the Barbary Corsairs*. I can also recommend *Thomas Jefferson and the Tripoli Pirates* by Brian Kilmeade and Don Yaeger along with Frederick C. Leiner's *The End of Barbary Terror*.

For the full story of Captain Eugene "Red" McDaniel's survival of the Hanoi Hilton, read his own account, written with James L. Johnson: *Scars & Stripes: The True Story of One Man's Courage in Facing Death as a Vietnam POW*.

If the story of Whittaker Chambers' sacrifice and dedication to our nation stirred something in you, you really should read it all in his own words, as so many people have said his writings are life-changing. Start with *Witness* and then his collected writings published under the title *Cold Friday*. A solid overview and introduction to the Chambers that I found useful was Daniel J. Mahoney's *Whittaker Chambers: Witness to the Crisis of the Modern Soul*, which can be found in the *Intercollegiate Review*, Spring 2002. And Richard M. Reinsch III's *Whittaker Chambers: The Spirit of a*

Counterrevolutionary is helpful in putting the man in his philosophical context.

On the eternal nature of war and the essentials of strategy, in addition to Clausewitz, Sun Tzu, and Machiavelli, I suggest a few modern titles:

Colin Gray: Modern Strategy

Edward N. Luttwak: *Strategy and Politics*

Hew Strachan: *Clausewitz's On War: A Biography*

Martin van Creveld: *The Culture of War*

Victor David Hanson: *The Western Way of War* and *The Second World Wars*

Carnes Lord: *The Modern Prince: What Machiavelli Can Teach us in the Age of Trump*

John Keegan: *History of Warfare* and *Strategy* (US Marine Corps publication MCDP 1-1, the 1991 version with introduction by General Krulak)

For a deeper analysis of the strategic challenges we face today, you can find most of my journal articles online. The best ones to start with are:

"How America Will Be Attacked: Irregular Warfare, the Islamic State, Russia, and China," *Military Review* (2016)

"The Islamic State and Information Warfare: Defeating ISIS and the Broader," (ed.), Threat Knowledge Group (2015)

"ISIS: The Threat to the United States," with Katharine Gorka, Threat Knowledge Group (2015)

"ISIS, Russia and Iran: The Role of Army Special Forces in the U.S. Response," (ed.) Threat Knowledge Group (2014)

"Know your Enemy," *Special Warfare*, Fort Bragg (2014)

"The Complexity Trap," with M. Gallagher and J. Geltzer, *Parameter* (2012)

"An Actor-Centric Theory of War," with David Kilcullen, *Joint Forces Quarterly* (2011)

"The Age of Irregular Warfare So What?" *Joint Forces Quarterly* (2010)

"Understanding History's Seven Stages of Jihad," *Sentinel* (2009)

On the threat we face from the global jihadi movement—groups like al-Qaeda and ISIS, and nations such as Iran—see my first book, *Defeating Jihad*, the professional text I co-authored and co-edited with the late Colonel Nick Pratt and Chris Harmon, *Toward a Grand Strategy Against Terrorism*, and my wife Katharine Gorka's book, *Fighting the Ideological War: Winning Strategies from Communism to Islamism*. Ayaan Hirsi Ali's *Infidel* is also essential reading for the broader context, as is Ibn Warraq's *Virgins? What Virgins?*, the superb *The Closing of the Muslim Mind* by Robert Reilly, and Bernard Lewis's *What Went Wrong: Western Impact and Middle Eastern Response*.

The subject of China is massive. Start with Michael Pillsbury's *The Hundred Year Marathon* and check out the excellent analyses by retired US Army Lt. Col. Tim Thomas of Fort Leavenworth's Foreign Military Affairs Office. For example, his presentation on current Chinese strategic thought. Additionally, follow the excellent writings of David Goldman, who writes the *Spengler* column online.

On what Russia is doing and what it plans to do next, there are few better than Ed Lucas of *The Economist*. See his book *The New Cold War: How the Kremlin Menaces Both Russia and the West* and his website, as well as the writings of Ilan Berman of the American Foreign Policy Council, who is also an authority on Iran and counterterrorism in general. From the practitioner's perspective, the writings of former CIA Moscow station chief Daniel Hoffman, who is now my colleague at Fox News, are excellent and can be found online at *The Hill* and Fox News.

To understand how the left gained control over American politics and culture, you have to read their master strategist, Saul Alinsky, who was Hillary Clinton's mentor and whose ideas Barack Obama studied and then taught in college. Read Alinsky's handbook *Rules for Radicals*, and then the late Andrew Breitbart's superb *Righteous Indignation: Excuse Me While I Save the World!*, which has the best summary I have read of the Gramscian infiltration of American politics and culture.

More details of the Left's radical evolution are provided by Bryan Burrough in *Days of Rage: America's Radical Underground, the FBI, and the Forgotten Age of Revolutionary Violence* and by Michael Walsh in *The Devil's Pleasure Palace*. See also the multiple works of David Horowitz. For example, his series *The Black Book of the American Left*.

Once you know what the enemy has in store for the republic, you need to know how best to respond. Go back to basics first with *Democracy in America* by Alexis de Tocqueville and *The Federalist Papers*. Place it all in the broader context of Judeo-Christian civilization with Rodney Stark's *How the West Was Won: The Neglected*

Start of the Triumph of Modernity and then read any of Mark Levin's crucial books on the defense of our Constitution and the republic.

Last, if you want to understand how we are again winning and taking back our nation, you must read Donald Trump's *The Art of the Deal*. Until, of course, my next book is out.

If you absorb all of the above, you will be part of the rebuilding and regeneration of the greatest nation on God's Earth.

America and Israel: Two Nations, One Destiny

America is a very special nation. So is Israel. There is a reason the phrase "Judeo-Christian civilization" starts with the word "Judeo."

The people of Israel are an ancient people whose history is chronicled in the most famous book there is and ever will be: the Bible.

The modern state of Israel was built against all odds by the survivors of the worst crime in all human history, the Holocaust, and a small group of other Jews who had been denied their homeland for centuries.

Today, with Donald J. Trump in the White House, we have the most pro-Israeli administration in America's short history. And this is a good thing. Because the Israeli people believe in what Americans believe in. They believe in individual liberty, in representative government, and the inherent dignity of all human beings as created in the image of God, and that is why they are our closest friends in the Middle East.

It was one of the high points of my time as Deputy Assistant and Strategist to President Trump to be asked to address the organization Christians United for Israel, on November 13, 2017, in the sixty-ninth year of Israel's rebirth.

Here I would like to share with you my thoughts on who Donald Trump really is, what his presidency means for Israel, why our bond is so deep, and the common enemies we face.

Let me start with a story of a young boy—a young boy who was nine years old when World War II broke out.

In the next six years, he saw his beloved city where he was born and raised, the beautiful city of Budapest, almost totally destroyed. He saw fascists take it over. He saw Nazi troops occupy the country and three out of every five buildings bombed by the end of the war.

During the war, after the fascist takeover, that young man would escort his schoolmates to school at the age of fourteen. He was born and raised a Catholic, but he had best friends at school who were forced to wear the Star of David by the Nazis because they were Jews. To stop them from being spat at and abused by the occupying Nazi forces, he would escort them every day to and from school. But then. it ended.

In 1945, Budapest was "liberated," and this young fifteen-year-old thought, "Now we have a chance." Why? Because he heard that the great men had sat down at Yalta and had come to an agreement, and they decided that countries like Hungary would finally, after years of devastation, be allowed to be free again, to choose their destiny as democracies, as free nations. So he had hope. But what happened?

Over the next three years, as this young boy grew to manhood, he saw his country not under the shackles of Nazis, but now under the shackles of another dictatorship—a communist dictatorship. The promises of Yalta were not to be. There would be no freedom. There would be a one-party state, and if you disagreed, you would be abused. You would be arrested and potentially disappear.

So what did he do? At the age of eighteen, when he started college, he said, "I'm going to resist the dictatorship. I've seen the fascists, and I don't like the communists. But I can't do it with a gun. I can't do it with bullets. I will do it quietly. I will do it secretly." He identified a small group of Christian students, patriots in college with him, and they collected sensitive information about what the Soviets were doing and how they were taking over Hungary. They smuggled that information out to the West, hoping that some nation could help them, use that information to liberate Hungary and the other captive nations behind the Iron Curtain. But the bad news was that when they finally connected with a foreign intelligence service, it was MI-6, and the coded missives that they were sending across the Iron Curtain were landing on the desk of one Kim Philby.

Kim Philby, as you may recall, was one of the five Cambridge Apostles, the deadliest traitors of the Cold War. Kim Philby collected the information, ran that group of young men for six months until he could identify every single one of them, and betrayed them to the KGB in Moscow and to the Hungarian Secret Police.

As a result, that man was arrested at the age of twenty and tortured by the secret police—in many cases, communist secret police, who just a few years earlier had been members of the Arrow Cross fascist regime. He was given a life sentence. He spent two years in a prison coal mine and two years in solitary. But then in 1956, his life changed when a group of young patriots captured a Soviet tank and, as part of the Hungarian Revolution, liberated that young man from that political prison. And with the seventeen-year-old daughter of a fellow prison inmate, he escaped to the West.

Now why do I tell you this story? I'm here to talk to you about America, Israel, and national security.

I tell you this story so you understand my perspective, because that man, of course, was my father. As a result of the history of my family, I look at the threat our two nations face today, and it is very easy to understand. There is a connective tissue between the Nazis of World War II, the communists of the Cold War, and groups like Hamas, Hezbollah, ISIS, and al-Qaeda. The connection is that they are all totalitarians. You cannot negotiate with Hitler, and you cannot negotiate with a jihadi. They will either kill you or enslave you. Or you will defeat them.

Today, you must have faith. Why? Because a man called Donald J. Trump is the president of the United States. Let me spend a couple of minutes telling you about who this man is. Oh, and by the way, "fake news" didn't begin in America. I think all our Israeli friends know where fake news started; fake news started in Israel. Fake news is not new to our Israeli friends, whether its articles are written about the Israeli Defense Forces or the BDS (boycott, divestment, sanctions) movement. Fake news may be new to Americans, but not to our friends in Israel.

So what do you need to know about Donald J. Trump?

Let me tell you a few things about the man and his team. I first met Mr. Trump when he invited me to New York in the summer of 2015 to come talk to him about national security issues in preparation for one of the Republican debates. What did I realize immediately about this man? This man is kryptonite to political correctness. Within seconds of our meeting, I immediately took a shine to this businessman from New York. Why? Because he had no time for political correctness. Secondly, he is a man who instantly communicated one thing to me: we, as a civilization, are at war. We stand for Judeo-Christian values, and we face a deadly enemy around the world who wishes to destroy those values. Not only did this man communicate that he understands we are at war—which was very refreshing, given the prior eight years— he also communicated the most important thing, which made me want to work for him. He wants to win that war.

What do you need to know about his team? Again, don't believe the fake news industrial complex. There are too many people out there who don't agree with the results of November 8, 2016, who would like to convince you that we run around the West Wing with our hair on fire. Not true. We laugh. We laugh at the coverage.

I remember one day coming in to Reince Priebus bent over a desk reading a newspaper with my boss, Steve Bannon, next to him, and they were belly laughing. And what were they laughing about? They said to each other, "Oh! Today you hate *me*? I thought I was supposed to hate *you*!" It doesn't even distract us. Why? Because in this White House, which will go down in history as the most pro-Israel White House *ever*, we have a job to do. We will reassert American leadership, and we will stand side by side with our allies and our closest friends, such as Israel, and we will win this war.

At this point, I must say thank you to all my friends out there, all our friends, the friends of the administration that have stood by us as we have been smeared mercilessly for months. The one thing that makes us realize they can never win is that when you look at who the people that tried to besmirch this president are—this president who has Orthodox Jewish grandchildren—just think about that for a moment—when you look at how they try to besmirch us, and when you look at what they have written in the past, you find a very, very interesting connection. The people who are most vile in their attacks against our administration are the same people who for years have supported President Obama's disastrous Iran deal and the BDS movement. Now isn't that interesting? Anti-Israeli attitudes today, such as the BDS movement, are the new anti-Semitism, and they should be treated as such.

So the president has an incredible team. What do you need to know about the president? Just a thumbnail sketch that I think I should share with you so you understand how that building really works. The president of the United States is a patriot. He loves this country. At the same time, he has a preternatural instinctual capability. This man's gut instincts are frightening to watch because they are always right. We spent hours in the Oval Office yesterday having a robust debate on the Iran Deal, and he was not happy with this very bad deal that we inherited from the former administration. And his gut reaction is always the right reaction. He can size you up in seconds. You give him a palette of options. He'll choose the right option almost instantly. That's the president, a man of unerringly correct instincts.

Now what is the threat we face? It's a significant threat, and here I'm just going to channel the boss. It's always good to quote the boss. I think in a few years, the Warsaw speech just given by the president will go down in history as one of the most important speeches ever given by a Western leader. Why? Because it's a reaffirmation of the first rule of warfare. There's a famous man called Sun Tzu. Everybody can quote Sun Tzu incorrectly. They always say, "Sun Tzu! Yes! He said, 'Know your enemy.'" No, he did not say, "Know your enemy." Sun Tzu, the ancient Chinese strategist, said, "If you know the enemy, you will win only half of your battles. If you want to win *all* your battles, if you want to win the war, you must not simply know who the enemy is, but you must know who *you* are and what you are fighting for."

The Warsaw speech was that moment. Why? Because what did the president say? At the site of the Warsaw uprising, in a country that lost twenty-five percent of its population during World War II, the president said the following: "The fundamental question of our time is whether the West has the will to survive. Do we have the confidence in our values to defend those values at any cost? Do we have the desire and the courage to preserve our civilization in the face of those who would subvert and destroy it?" He went on to say, "Our fight for the West does not begin on the battlefield. It begins in our minds, in our wills. It begins in our souls."

The president, in Warsaw, reaffirmed who we are. He reaffirmed the values of our civilization, built upon Judeo-Christian heritage, the belief that we are made in the image of our Creator. That's where our dignity comes from, that we believe in an objective truth. There is no relativism; there is no subjectivity about the truth. There is no, "Well the terrorist could have a point of view." No, they endanger us, whether at a bus station in Tel Aviv or a nightclub in Orlando, Florida.

The key point here is that America's enemies are Israel's enemies. Israel's enemies are our enemies. As the vice president said on the Day of National Independence for Israel—I was there when he said it—"Under President Trump, let me assure all of you, if the world knows one thing, it must know that America stands with Israel. Her cause is our cause. Her values are our values. Her fight is our fight."

What is the bond between our two great nations? Here I'm going to steal from a good friend of mine. Jeff, if you're out there listening, you know who you are. Jeff shared with me a sentence—he might have stolen it from somebody else—but it was a wonderful sentence. "America is the greatest nation man ever made; Israel is the greatest God ever made."

At the end of the day, we understand, the president understands, and his team understands, that we will both be safe when the black flag of jihad, the black flag of ISIS, is as universally reviled across the world as the swastika is today.

Then, we will have won. Thank you.

Who Are the Jihadis?

We are still fighting the jihadis that were behind the largest terrorist attack in modern history. Al-Qaeda may have lost its headquarters in Afghanistan, and the Islamic State may have lost its "caliphate" now that Donald J. Trump is America's commander in chief, but the final act in our war with the global jihadi movement has yet to play out.

Before coming to the White House, one of the highest honors I had was to serve as an expert for the prosecution in the trial of the Boston Marathon bomber, Dzhokhar Tsarnaev.

My task was to demonstrate that the younger surviving bomber was not a pawn of his older brother, but a fully-fledged and willing member of the jihadi movement.

To that end, I was allowed unprecedented access to all the jihadist materials the FBI had discovered on Tsarnaev's laptop so I could write a report on who he was, what he believed, and why he did what he did on that horrific day in Boston.

This report has never been published before.

It will help you understand whom we face, what they are planning, and what it will take to defeat them.

UNITED STATES V. DZHOKHAR TSARNAEV EXPERT REPORT OF DR. SEBASTIAN L. GORKA SUMMARY

This report is based upon my twenty-three years of experience in counterterrorism and academic analysis of terrorism as applied to the documents supplied to me by the US Attorney's Office for the District of Massachusetts as part of the case of *US v. Dzhokhar* Tsarnaev.

In the report, I cover:

- The characteristics and evolution of the modern Global Jihadist Movement.
- Key concepts of the Jihadist Movement and how they apply to its use of terrorism.
- The role of Jihadist media and the use of the internet to recruit and radicalize individuals to become terrorists, and to disseminate the techniques and tradecraft used in terrorist attacks.
- The way in which the Jihadist Movement has exploited geopolitical events around the world.
- The significance of evidence found in the possession of the accused as related to the Jihadist Movement and acts of terrorism.

As will be seen, my conclusion is that the defendant, Dzhokhar Tsarnaev, identified with, and considered himself to be a part of, the Global Jihadist Movement, and that he executed terrorist attacks in furtherance of and in accordance with the movement's declared objectives.

This conclusion is based upon the very large library of extremist materials (two thousand-plus pages, as well as numerous audio and video files) in the possession of the defendant, and most importantly, upon documents he himself wrote.

The pivotal such document that clearly indicates Tsarnaev's conscious identification with the Jihadist Movement is the statement he left in the boat where he was found to be hiding after the Boston Marathon bombings.

The Defendant's written statement is clearly informed by the jihadist concept of *al wala al barra*, which stipulates that a Muslim owes no allegiance to, and must not obey the laws of, any political system that is not run by Muslims, and that such un-Islamic systems must be destroyed.

EXPERIENCE

I am the Major General Matthew C. Horner Distinguished Chair of Military Theory at the Marine Corps University, a privately endowed, non-governmental position. I teach and conduct executive research on terrorism, counterterrorism, and the grand strategy of Jihadism.

Prior to taking the Horner Chair, I was on the faculty of the National Defense University for six years, eventually serving as the Associate Dean of Congressional Affairs and Relations to the Special Operations Community. As such, I was part of the International Counterterrorism Fellowship Program of the Department of Defense, which provides graduate-level education and partnership capacity-building to the interagency and US allies and partners involved in the global campaign against al-Qaeda and Associated Movements (AQAM).

For four years before coming to the US, I was on the faculty of the Program for Terrorism and Security Studies at the George C. Marshall Center, US European Command, where I was involved in the counterterrorism education and training of over one thousand counterterrorism and intelligence officers from around the world.

Although I am now a US citizen, when I lived in the United Kingdom, I served in the British Territorial Army's Intelligence and Security Group (V), which was a reserve military unit with counterterrorism responsibilities.

In addition to my position with the Marine Corps University, I am currently an Adjunct Professor with Georgetown University and an Associate Fellow with Joint Special Operations University, US Special Operations Command (SOCOM). I am a lead instructor for SOCOM's Special Operations Combating Terrorism Course, and teach on two other SOCOM counterterrorism courses. I am also a regular instructor for the US Army Special Operations Command's John F. Kennedy Special Warfare Center and School, where I teach the block "Thinking Like a Jihadist Terrorist." I also teach for the Counterterrorism Division of the FBI on their Joint Terrorism Task Force and Counterterrorism Operations courses, and I am course designer and director for the FBI's Terrorism: Origins and Ideologies course.

I have published in excess of 180 monographs, book chapters, and journal articles on national security, and terrorism more specifically. These include for *Janes Terrorism Monitor* and *Janes Islamic Affairs Analyst*, as well as the *Harvard International Review*, and *Special Warfare*, the official periodical of the US Special Forces. I am contributing co-editor of the McGraw Hill text: *Toward a Grand Strategy against Terrorism*, and have testified before Congress on the global campaign against the Jihadist Movement and have briefed the same topic for the CIA and the Office of the Director of National Intelligence.

My undergraduate degree in philosophy and theology was from London University. I was a post-graduate fellow at Harvard's Kennedy School of Government and I have a Ph.D. in political science from Corvinus University, Budapest. My dissertation was on the difference between politically- and religiously-motivated terrorism and the consequences for national security policy.

THE EVOLUTION OF THE MODERN JIHADIST MOVEMENT

Jihad is a concept central to the religion of Islam. It can refer to many different activities from *striving* to live a good life without sin, to martial *fighting* against unbelievers.

With regard to the latter usage, who constitutes an unbeliever can vary greatly.[1] Historically, the targets of violent jihad have ranged from Arab tribes who rebelled against the early caliphs to the leaders of the Muslim community themselves when they were deemed to be un-Islamic. In the latter instances, when "believers" used force against those who also called themselves Muslims, the principle of *takfir* was often invoked. Associated predominantly with the scholar Taqi ad-Din A mad ibn Taymiyyah, *takfirism* is the widespread use of the accusation that a Muslim has, by his or her actions, committed apostasy and is therefore no longer a true Muslim and must be killed.

In the twentieth century, geopolitical events helped catalyze a modernization and reconceptualization of jihad by several key authors and politico-religious leaders employing modern takfirism. This eventually resulted in the establishment of today's Global Jihadist Movement and terrorist groups such as al-Qaeda.

The Jihadist Movement is inexorably tied to the idea of the *caliphate*, or the theocratic empire of Islam, that was established by the founder of the religion, Abū al-Qāsim Muhammad ibn 'Abd Allāh ibn 'Abd al Muttalib ibn Hāshim, also known as Mohammad.

The caliphate, which had been established and was then enlarged very rapidly after the founding of Islam, stretching from Southern Spain to Central Asia and beyond, lasted as a politico-religious entity for over a millennium, controlled by different dynasties, and headquartered variously in Mecca, Damascus, Baghdad, and Istanbul.

The caliphate's most modern version, lasting into the twentieth century, was the Ottoman Empire. This embodiment of the theocratic regime of Islam faced an existential threat after it decided to side with the forces of Germany and the Austro-Hungarian Empire in World War I but then lost the war.

In order to prevent the forcible partition of the whole caliphate, the Ottomans decided to reinvent and reform the Islamic Empire into the modern secularized republic of Turkey under the leadership of Mustafa Kemal Ataturk. The most significant part of the modernization process, from the point of view of modern jihad, was the formal dissolution of the caliphate by the government of Istanbul in 1924.

With the new Turkish government forcibly separating mosque and state in a new secular republic, the loss of the theocratic character of the thousand-plus year old successor entity to the empire would become a cause for violence to those who saw the decision as a triumph of heretical western values over the non-negotiable attributes of Islam.

Most influential among such actors was Hassan al-Banna, the founder of the *Ikwaan al Muslimeen*, or Muslim Brotherhood (MB). Established in the Suez region of Egypt less than five years after the dissolution of the caliphate, the Brotherhood had as it mandate the re-establishment of the theocratic Empire through subversion of existing local governmental regimes and through Holy War (jihad).

This is best demonstrated by the official motto of the Brotherhood:

> *Allah is our goal.*
> *The Prophet is our leader.*
> *The Quran is our constitution.*
> *Jihad is our way.*
> *Death in the service of Allah is the loftiest of our wishes.*[2]

With the persistent waning of Western colonial control in the Middle East and North Africa in the years after World War I and

World War II, the Muslim Brotherhood grew in influence across the region, often in ways that threatened the newly independent governments that had been established after the withdrawal of the Western powers. As a result, the MB was frequently suppressed or outlawed and its leaders imprisoned or executed by the new post-colonial governments of the Arab and Muslim world.

Second in importance only to al-Banna himself is the Muslim Brotherhood strategist and author Sayyid Qutb.

A minor official in the Egyptian Ministry of Education in the 1950s, he came to the United States on an exchange program to study our school system. After spending two years in the US, he concluded that America represents a godless and materialist civilization antithetical to all that is good in Islam and that it must be destroyed.

Returning to Cairo, he decided to provide the answer to how this destruction must be wrought and why. Chief amongst the works he wrote which to this very day shapes and influences the Jihadist Movement around the world is the slim text *Milestones*.[3]

Key to Qutb's argument is the belief that Islam has lost its way and that only war can purify the Muslim community and win back greatness for Islam and glory for Allah.

According to the author, the world is once again in a state of pagan ignorance of the one true god, a state that the Koran refers to a *jahalliyyah*. In fact, the situation is so dire that Qutb is adamant that no one state existing today is truly Islamic. They have all been subverted by the materialism endemic in their societies and the invidious influence of the un-Islamic values of the West.

Additionally, Qutb saw democracy itself as a great threat to the sovereignty of Islam. In a democracy men make laws over other men and that is the same as dictatorship, according to Qutb. What is more, Islam is quite explicit in his reading, in that there can only ever be one legislator: Allah. As a result of the dictatorial nature of democracy and the fact that democratic systems by definition abrogate the authority of the creator, Qutb decreed that all democracies must be destroyed.[4]

Together, the ideas of al-Banna and Qutb and key regional events in the first half of the twentieth century laid the the foundation for a reconceptualization of jihad for the modern era. This reconceptualization would be operationalized by events in 1979 that would see the creation of an international Jihadist Movement and the conditions for the eventual establishment of global terrorist groups such as al-Qaeda.

The year 1979 marked a turn of century in the Arab/Islamic world given their use of the lunar-based *hijra* calendar. 1979 in the Middle East and for Muslims everywhere represented the move from the year 1399 hijra to the year 1400 hijra. As with most civilizations, the advent of a new century was met with great expectation, with the belief in the likelihood of significant events associated with the new year 1400. Indeed, the year would see three very significant occurrences.

The first happened in the Shia world and was the Iranian Revolution. The importance of the fall of the Shah's regime's and its replacement by the Ayatollah and theocratic Supreme Council cannot be overestimated and is not limited to the Persian community or Shia world.

With its core message of a revolution meant to utterly reject the Western model of governance and its separation of "church and state," the events in Tehran in 1979 still stand as a clarion call to all who wish to see Islamic theocracy re-established and who believe that democracy is *haram*, or forbidden, and that a Muslim may only live in an Islamic state and under (Islamic) sharia law.

The fact that this Shia-led theocratic and revolutionary state still challenges the West today acts as a catalyst and source of motivation for Sunni fundamentalists as well, such as those found in al-Qaeda. Both Sunni and Shia extremists agree on the need for theocracy. Where they differ is on the question of who should be in control and which version of the religion will inform the theocracy, Shiism or Sunni Islam.

The second event of the "new" century occurred on the very first day of the new Islamic year, *Murrham* 01 1400, or November 20, 1979. On that day, several thousand jihadist terrorists armed with automatic weapons laid siege to, and captured, the holiest site in Islam, the Grand Mosque of Mecca. This event, which shocked not only the Kingdom of Saudi Arabia but also the broader Islamic world, would have ramifications for international, religiously-informed terrorism that are still felt today.

The jihadists had come to the conclusion that the Muslim world was so corrupted by lack of fealty to Allah and the influence of heretical Western values that it could only be cleansed and returned to greatness by a purifying Holy War, or jihad. First among the target of the terrorists was the government of Saudi Arabia itself and the royal House of Saud which was deemed to be a puppet regime of the West and in a state of apostasy.[5]

Given the fact that the official title for the monarch of the Kingdom of Saudi Arabia is the Protector of the Two Holy Sites (Mecca and Medina), the assault was especially damaging for the then King and his royal house. This damage was later compounded when it was discovered that the terrorists had been endorsed and blessed in their assault against the "apostate House of Saud" by numerous members of the Saudi *ulema*, or clerical class.[6]

After almost two weeks, the jihadists were finally killed or captured, but the siege of the Grand Mosque established an example for those who wished to rebuild a new, purer Islam and use deadly force to do so.

The last and most operationally important event in 1979, from the point of view of the future al-Qaeda and the internationalization of the Jihadist Movement, was the Soviet invasion of Afghanistan. Although technically a socialist state, Afghanistan was historically Muslim and thus fell into the category of *Dar al Islam*, or permanently Muslim territory. As such, when it was invaded without provocation by the troops of a Western and atheistic state, the USSR, this doctrinally necessitated *defensive jihad* to re-establish Muslim rule and expel the infidel invaders.

A Palestinian cleric from Jordan named Abdullah Azzam, who had a Ph.D. in Islamic Studies and Jurisprudence from the most important Sunni theological institution in the world, the Al Azhar in Cairo, decided to become part of the effort to liberate Afghanistan from the infidel.[7]

Azzam decided that without external help, the outnumbered Afghans would not be able to resist the Soviet forces. As a result, he established the anodyne sounding Services Bureau (*Maktab al Khidamat*), or MAK. The MAK, based first in Pakistan and later in Afghanistan itself, was an organization for recruiting and training non-Afghans (*Arab Mujahedeen*) to become holy warriors in the war against the occupying infidel forces of the USSR.

Azzam travelled the world with a message of fighting back against the persecution of Muslims, attracting Egyptians, Yemenis, Jordanians, and Saudis, among others, to come and join the "holy war" against the infidel invaders. One of the Saudi Arabians attracted to the cause, and who would later become Azzam's deputy, was Osama bin Laden. It should be noted that of the jihadist texts found in the defendant's possession, Azzam's are the most numerous.

Azzam should be appreciated as the individual who most internationalized and popularized the modern conceptualization of Jihad. His 1979 fatwa, or religious decree, *Defense of Muslim Lands*,[8] also in the possession of the Defendant, is a seminal jihadist document and remains so within the Global Jihadist Movement.

In it, Azzam states that *Jihad*, holy war, is now *fard 'ayn*, an individual and universal obligation of all believers. His logic for doing so is clear and his Ph.D. from Al Azhar gives the document the true weight of an official fatwa, or religious decree.

Azzam's argument is that with the Soviet invasion of Muslim territory, and Muslim lives under threat from the infidel, Holy War is required. However an official response on behalf of the global

Muslim community will not be automatically forthcoming given that President Ataturk of Turkey dissolved the caliphate in 1924. As a result of that decision there is no Islamic Empire or Emperor (caliph) left to declare a retaliatory war or to provide command authority for a military action against the infidel invaders. As a result, it is incumbent upon *all Muslims* to act individually in the name of Islam to protect the faith and their co-religionists.

Azzam is also very specific with the wording of his fatwa. He states that all Muslims, no matter where they live, rich or poor, must fulfill this religious obligation. One of the first to do so was Osama bin Laden, Azzam's future deputy in the MAK who, when Azzam was assassinated ten years later in Pakistan, would inherit the whole organization and rename it *al-Qaeda al Jihad*, the Base for Holy War.

The last significant occurrence of 1979 came with the publication of a book on jihad by a general in the Pakistani armed forces. The *Quranic Concept of War*[9] by Brigadier S. K. Malik is unlike any modern book by a Western military author and can be taken as a synthesis of Islamic military strategy and a religious justification of terrorist violence.

Endorsed by the then President of Pakistan, General Zia ul Haq, and the equivalent of the then attorney general of Pakistan, the text reinforces Azzam's fatwa that Holy War is an obligation of all Muslims before going on to provide a three-part argument on what the purpose of war actually is and how it should be waged against the *kuffar*, or infidel.

The text opens with a repudiation of Western military thought as embodied in the foundational work of the Prussian strategist Carl von Clausewitz. Clausewitz's groundbreaking text *On War* has as its theme the idea that war is simply "the continuation of politics by other means." In other words, that war is a function of the modern nation-state whereby national interests are realized when other means, such as diplomacy or economic measures, fail.

In the first part of Malik's work, this Western understanding of the purpose of war is completely rejected. Instead, the General writes that *all wars may only serve one purpose, and this purpose alone: the realization of Allah's sovereignty on the Earth.*

Secondly, Malik also rejects the Western practice of looking for multiple "centers-of-gravity" or key vulnerabilities to attack within the enemy during wartime. Instead he states unequivocally that when fighting the enemies of Allah, one should not look for multiple targets such as command centers, resupply routes, or logistics hubs. According to Malik, there is only one target in the enemy that counts, and it isn't even a physical one. According to *The Quranic Concept of War, the only target in war that matters at all is the soul of the infidel. The believer must convert them to Islam or kill them.*

The last portion of the jihadist text is the most pertinent to the current threat of jihadi terrorism and events such as the bombing of the Boston marathon. In it, Malik states that *since the soul of the infidel is the only target that matters in war, the most effective mode of attack is terror.* As a result, terrorism is the best tool to use against the non-Muslim, or infidel.

THE OBJECTIVES OF THE GLOBAL JIHADIST MOVEMENT

Based upon the works of al-Banna, Qutb, Azzam, and Malik, and the pronouncements of other jihadist strategists and writers to include Anwar al-Awlaki and Abu Muhammad Asim al-Maqdisi, which were also found in the Defendant's possession, the objectives of the modern Global Jihadist Movement can be summarized as follows:

- To violently eradicate pagan ignorance of Allah (*jahalliyyah*) from the world.
- To eject foreign militaries and Western influences from Muslim lands (*Dar al Islam*).

- To destroy all un-Islamic political systems, especially Western democracies.
- To re-establish the theocratic empire of Islam, the caliphate.

The "true believer" must follow the way of *al wala al barra*.[10] He or she must reject those things which are un-Islamic and by his or her actions show loyalty to Allah. The nature of the acts taken in further-ance of Islam and for the good of Allah are bounded by the context of the believer. If they live in Dar al Islam, territory that is ruled by Islamic leaders and in accordance with sharia, they must defend that territory from un-Islamic infidel influence or they must travel to those places where their coreligionists are at war with the infidel, or to the heart of the enemy, as the al-Qaeda operatives did on September 11, 2001, and wreak havoc within the center of disbelief.

If the believer is living in *Dar al-Harb*—literally *The House of War*—they must chose between *hijra* or *jihad*. *They must emigrate to Muslim lands or destroy the un-Islamic system in which they find themselves.*

In the case of the defendant, these elements were combined. His family background in Russia contained the elements of a Muslim community ruled and persecuted by an un-Islamic leadership—the infidel regime in Moscow—and at the personal level, with the move of the Tsarnaev family to the US, the defendant was in the position to have to choose between emigration to a Muslim land or jihad against the infidel state in which he lived.

If the latter is chosen, then the narrative of the Jihadist Movement is clear that the violent actions taken should include terrorist acts designed to maximize civilian casualties.[11] The theme here is that the suffering of Muslims around the world at the hands of the infidel must be avenged through the suffering of those "punished" through terrorist attack.[12]

Closing this ideological progression is the narrative's guarantee of salvation. Those that embark on Jihad are described as qualitatively better than other believers, and those that die in the performance of Jihad, who become *shaheed*, or martyrs to Islam, will achieve paradise and enjoy eternal rewards in the highest levels of heaven.[13] This latter theme of the rewards the shaheed will enjoy is covered at great length by the series of lectures by the al-Qaeda leader Anwar al Awlaki entitled *Hereafter,* which were also consumed by the defendant.

KEY CONCEPTS OF THE GLOBAL JIHADIST MOVEMENT AND LEXICON OF RELEVANT TERMS

There are numerous Arabic words which apply to and recur within the literature of the Jihadist Movement and which are central to the concepts used to recruit members to acts of violence and to justify those acts religiously. The most important include:

Al wala al barra: the concept of being loyal to that which pleases Allah, and renouncing or subverting that which does not please Allah. This is used by the Jihadist Movement to explain to its members that a "true" believer must not be loyal to an un-Islamic system, and if he does not leave that system he must subvert and destroy it. This is the choice between *hijra* and *jihad*.

Caliphate: the theocratic Empire of Islam established by Mohammad in Mecca which grew rapidly and changed its center to Damascus and Baghdad, and finally was headquartered in the early twentieth century in Istanbul, and known as the Ottoman Empire. Dissolved and replaced by the secular Turkish Republic under President Mustafa Kemal Ataturk, both the Muslim Brotherhood and the Global Jihadist Movement have as their strategic objective the re-establishment of the caliphate.

Fard 'ayn: an individual and universal obligation upon all Muslims, as applied to *Jihad* by Abdullah Azzam and others.

Firdaws: the highest level of *Jannah*, the Muslim paradise. This level is reserved for the most righteous to include the prophets of Islam and martyrs to the faith, the *shaheed*.

Hijra: the journey undertaken by Mohammad to the city of Yathrib (latterly Medina) after he began to proselytize but was rejected by the pagan Arab tribes in Mecca. The word hijra has been developed by jihadi extremists to describe the experience of a believer being rejected by an un-Islamic society, being forced into the hardship of a forced emigration, only to eventually find recognition after success in Jihad.

Islamism: is the word used to describe the modern belief that Muslims must live under Islamic systems that are theocratic, such as systems of governance that reintegrate politics and Islam as per the system created originally by Mohammad.

Jihad: can be used to refer to the striving of a believer against temptation or that which is forbidden (*haram*), or to physical war against the non-believer (*kuffar*). For the Global Jihadist Movement, Holy War, or Jihad, is an individual obligation of all Muslims which will bring about a cleansing of the world and the re-establishment of the caliphate.

Kuffar / Kufr: the non-believer or infidel / Non-belief. This can refer to the Atheist, Christian, or Jew, but also to the Muslim who has denied Islam and is therefore an apostate and must be killed.

Jahalliyyah: originally used to describe the pagan and idolatrous state of ignorance of the tribes of the Arabian Peninsula prior to the establishment of the caliphate, this word is used by leaders of the Jihadist Movement to describe the lack of faith in the world today, especially among nominal Muslim communities who no longer submit themselves to the will of Allah.

Jahannam: the word for Hell in Islam, consisting of several levels with their own gates, each for a different degree of sinner.

Jannah: the Muslim equivalent of heaven, the paradise of the after-life consisting of numerous levels for the various grades of those rewarded.

Qiyamat: the word used to refer to the Day of Resurrection in Islam. Analogous to Judgment Day in End Times.

Shahada: the first 'pillar' of Islam, the declaration whereby a Muslim formally becomes a member of the *ummah*, the global community of Islam, by asserting that: "There is but one God; Allah is his name; and Mohammad is his Messenger."

The Black Flag of the Shahada: the black banner bearing in white the Arabic text of the *Shahada* as used by al-Qaeda and other terrorist groups such as ISIS/The Islamic State.

Shaheed: Martyr to Islam, the person who dies fighting the infidel in furtherance of Islam. Used specifically by the Global Jihadist Movement to recruit terrorists with the narrative that those who have died in Holy War will be greatly rewarded in heaven.

JIHADIST USE OF THE MEDIA AND THE INTERNET

The Office of the United States Attorney for the District of Massachusetts supplied me with electronic materials related to al-Qaeda and the Jihadist Movement found in the possession of the defendant. These include dozens of e-books, jihadist *nasheeds* (Islamic chants), and video lectures from al-Qaeda leaders such as Anwar al Awlaki, as well as seven issues of the English language extremist publication *Inspire* magazine produced by al-Qaeda in the Arabian Peninsula under the editorship of Samir Khan.

Given its significance in particular to the techniques and methods employed in the bombing of the Boston Marathon, I will here discuss the first issue of *Inspire* magazine and how its content connects to the Boston attack.

The first issue of al-Qaeda's Jihadist magazine opens with a Letter from the Editor explaining who the audience for the publication is:

"This Islamic Magazine is geared towards making the Muslim a mujahid in Allah's path."

The publication is then described as "the first magazine to be issued by the al-Qaʿidah Organization in the English language."[14]

The issue goes on to praise the terrorist actions of Umar Farouk Abdulmutallab, the Christmas Day bomber:[15]

"We call on every Muslim who feels any jealousy for their religious beliefs to expel the polytheists from the Arabian Peninsula, by killing all of the crusaders working in embassies or otherwise, and to declare war against the crusaders in the land of the Prophet Muhammad - peace be upon him - on the ground, sea and air."

"Hence, we say to the American people: as you support your leaders and are standing behind them to kill our women and children, rejoice for what is coming to you! We will come to you with slaughter and have prepared men who love death as you love life, and with the permission of Allah we will come to you with something you cannot handle. As you have killed us, so shall you be killed, and that tomorrow for its seeker is close."

This is followed by personal messages from Osama bin Laden, the then head of al-Qaeda, and Ayman al-Zawahiri, his deputy and the future head of the terror group.[16]

Most significant of all for the purposes of this case, is the section of the magazine entitled *Open Source Jihad*.[17] This will be a recurring section in future issues of *Inspire* and is described as a "resource manual for those who loathe the tyrants; includes bomb making techniques, security measures, guerrilla tactics, weapons training, and all other jihadi related activities" and "It allows Muslims to train at home instead of risking a dangerous travel abroad."

The section includes the now infamous article: *Make a Bomb in the Kitchen of Your Mom*,[18] which provides detailed instructions on how to prepare an improvised explosive device (IED), how to make detonators, primary charges, improvised timers for delayed detonation, and how to make such devices as lethal as possible through the use of nails and other metal ingredients to act as shrapnel. Note the explicit wording:

> "The inflammable substance needs to be contained in a strong container that would allow the pressure to build up and thus cause a damaging explosion."

The author recommends pressure cookers as the most effective container for the improvised explosive with shrapnel glued to the inside, and for maximum destructive effect advises that the device be placed "in a crowded area."[19]

The terrorist tradecraft section then provides instructions or how to use commercially available encryption keys to secure Jihadist communications and prevent detection by law enforcement, and gives advice on how to blend into one's surrounding and immerse oneself in local (infidel) culture to avoid detection.

Near the end of the magazine comes an article by Anwar al-Awlaki himself, the individual considered to be the main driver behind *Inspire*. Entitled: *Shaykh Anwar's Message to the America People and the Muslims of the West*,[20] it includes the statement:

> "I for one, was born in the US, and lived in the US for 21 years. America was my home. I was a preacher of Islām involved in non-violent Islāmic activism. However, with the American invasion of Iraq and continued US aggression against Muslims, I could not reconcile between living in the US and being a Muslim, and I eventually came to the

conclusion that jihād against America is binding upon myself, just as it is binding on every other able Muslim."

Discussing the Fort Hood terrorist attack, he describes its perpetrator, Major Nidal Hasan, as using violence in response to actions of the US government:

"Ni āl Ḥassan [sic] was not recruited by al-Qā'idah; Ni āl Ḥassan was recruited by American crimes, and this is what America refuses to admit. America refuses to admit that its foreign policies are the reason behind a man like Ni āl Ḥassan, born and raised in the US, turning his guns against American soldiers. And the more crimes America commits, the more mujāhidīn will be recruited to fight against it."

Most significantly, Awlaki gives a very operational choice to Muslims living in un-Islamic countries such as America, a choice based upon the principle of *al wala al barra*. He tells the Muslims of America and the West:

"To the Muslims in America I have this to say: How can your conscience allow you to live in peaceful coexistence with a nation that is responsible for the tyranny and crimes committed against your own brothers and sisters? How can you have your loyalty to a government that is leading the war against Islām and Muslims?"[21]

"Hence, my advice to you is this: you have two choices: either hijra [migration] or jihād. You either leave or you fight. You leave and live among Muslims or you stay behind and fight with your hand, your wealth and your word. I specifically invite the youth to either fight in the West or join their brothers in the fronts of jihād: Afghanistan, Iraq, and Somalia."[22]

This message of leave un-Islamic lands or fight is reinforced by the one-page document found in the Defendant's possession entitled: *Jihad: The Forgotten Obligation.* This states univocally that:

- There is "no deed equivalent to Jihad."
- That Holy War is "the obligatory act."
- The most virtuous deed is Jihad.
- Other deeds cannot compete with Jihad.
- The person who does Jihad in Allah's path is superior to other Muslims.

The Office of the US Attorney also supplied me with over sixty-five audio or video files consumed by the defendant. These represent a significant collection of Jihadist materials and below are the details of the files most relevant to the bombing of the Boston Marathon.

Aseer nasheed: this is an audio and video file which uses the Islamic chant or *nasheed* format to disseminate the Jihadist Movement's call to violence in the face of perceived oppression.

The audio track is, in the YouTube file accessed by the defendant, combined with a series of images and written statements. The opening images of the video are of men in Islamic dress being held in prison, in confinement. The nasheed speaks to the observers' feeling restless as if they are the actual captives and continues with the following words displayed on the screen:

> *This feeling of humiliation is surrounding me, as I see our heroes being chained by the worthless (disbelievers)* [this is accompanied but what appears to be an image of Guantanamo detainees] *I am imprisoned O my Lord, without any guilt (except determination), motivated by the call of Jihad* [these words being superimposed over an image of Omar Abdel Rahman, also known as the Blind Sheikh,

who is currently serving a life sentence in relation to the 1993 World Trade Center bombing.]

Then the following text is displayed:

O my Lord! The one who is Almighty over the people
  People whose oppression no words can describe
  [with the image of US soldiers amongst civilians in either Iraq or Afghanistan],
  And have patience O captive you are free
  To the hereafter you will go without any chains....
  The video continues:
  O unshakeable one ... you will roar and you will revenge for that sake of Allah (swt) [subhanahu wa ta' ala / Glory to him the exalted]

This is followed by a still shot of a poster with the words:

What can my enemies do to me?
  I have in my breast both my heavan (sic) and my garden.
  If I travel they are with me, never leaving me.
  Imprisonment for me is a chance to be alone with my Lord.
  To be killed is martyrdom & to be exiled from my land is a spiritual journey,

It continues:

And the hope of the heroes is to live with dignity
  And if they die then Jannah [paradise/heaven] *and Hurul'een* [chaste females] *await*
  And the hope of the heroes is to live with dignity.

This is accompanied by three photos of Abu Hamza al Masri and the superscript: *May Allah (SWT), Free our Brother in Islam.*

Abu Hamza, also known as Kamel Mustafa, was the UK-based radical cleric extradited to the US and convicted earlier this year of material support to terrorism.[23] This is followed by the words: *"And if they die then Jannah and Hurul'een wait"* and a picture of Ali al-Timimi with the superscript: *May Allah (SWT) Release our Beloved Sheikh from the hands of the Kaffireen* [Infidels].

Al-Timimi was convicted of enlisting individuals to wage war against the United States in the *Virginia Jihadi Network* trial of 2005.[24]

The defendant also consumed material concerning "Commander Khattab," a Saudi national whose real name was Thamir Saleh Abdullah Al-Suwailem. He is significant insofar as he was a key figure in not only the mujahedeen resistance against the Soviets in Afghanistan in the 1980s, but also in the First and Second Chechen wars against the Russian Federation.

The *Commander Khattab* video file[25] is a hagiographic representation of the Jihadist's life in the form of a nasheed with numerous battlefield images, including Khattab with a surface to air man-portable missile system (MANPAD).

Khattab was one of the most important figures in the international Jihadist Movement who in the 1980s was an associate of Osama bin Laden and a leader of the *Islamic International Brigade* which he established in 1998 with Shamil Basayev.[26] Later he would become the head of the *Arab Mujahedeen in Chechnya* (also known as *Ansar in Chechnya*). As such he was involved in establishing training camps in southeastern Chechnya, "which trained unemployed young Chechen men and Muslims from throughout Russia for a jihad that was far greater in scope than originally envisioned by Chechnya's nationalist leadership."[27]

The nasheed *When will the Muslim ummah unite?* was presented as being in the possession of the defendant in both video and audio format.

The video[28] and accompanying voiceover is a highly compressed version of the key elements of the Jihadist Movement's narrative. It opens by describing the 1924 dissolution of the Islamic Empire, the caliphate, as a catastrophe after which the West invaded Islamic territories and:

> [P]ledged us to useless flags and brought the kuffar [infidels] to our lands.

Then the nasheed speaks of the Western culture of which the Muslims "became instant fans" and how they abandoned their religion "so Allah abandoned us." It continues as follows:

> So when we strayed from Islam a wake-up call we were handed.
> And the troops of the devils in our nations quickly landed to colonize the Muslims
> The worst amongst us were made to lead us
> They too were oppressors and didn't even feed us.
> This is followed by:
> The time is for Jihad and Salaam [Peace] to the believers who participate.
> We stand humiliated until we rethink our aims
> We are here to reestablish Islam on this Earth
> So by the will of Allah let's give Islam a rebirth
> The video closes with a passage from the Koran (4:95):
> Not equal are those of the believers who sit (at home), except those who are disabled,
> and those who strive hard and fight in the cause of Allah
> with their wealth and their lives.
> Allah has preferred in grades those who strive hard and fight

with their wealth and their lives above those who sit (at home).

Unto each, Allah has promised good (paradise),
but Allah has preferred those whose strive hard and fight,
above those who sit (at home), by a huge reward.

The audio file *The Man who went to Jannah* [heaven] *without Praying* is a brief recounting of a tale in which a man is fatally wounded in battle. The significance of the story is that the man had never prayed to Allah or even fasted in the manner prescribed by the "Pillars of Islam." Nevertheless, the story ends with the otherwise un-Islamic individual being rewarded with life in jannah, or heaven, because when asked before his death whether he fought "for the sake of Islam," he answered, "Yes." As such he qualified as a *shaheed*, a martyr of Islam, and is rewarded with entry into paradise.

The narrator concludes by noting that being a martyr to Islam "is the one deed that would guarantee a person the highest level of jannah without doing anything else."

The last two files are the *Rasool Allah Inspiring Words Of Truth!* and *Rasool Allah The Prophet Of Mercy And War!*

The first is a harsh critique of the way Muslims currently live their lives and is a call for believers to understand the depth of their responsibilities as Muslims.

The speaker identifies the most frightening part of the Koran as the one which deals with Judgment Day, when all the actions of each person will be judged and all will be held accountable. In the last part of this first file, the audience is reminded that Mohammad said, "I am the one that will wipe the kuffar [infidel] from the face of this Earth."

The second file has the same speaker talking over the sounds of battle quoting Mohammad again as saying: "I am the prophet of Jihad. I am the prophet of massacre," and exhorting his audience not to follow the middle way, not to simply avoid that which is *haram* [forbidden] and at the same time take no action to establish the caliphate, since "Islam should dominate," and it is the believer's responsibility to be at the "forefront" of this effort and make it a reality.

THE SIGNIFICANCE OF EVIDENCE FOUND IN THE POSSESSION OF THE ACCUSED AS RELATED TO THE JIHADIST MOVEMENT AND ACTS OF TERRORISM

Even if the Boston bombing had not occurred, or if the documents belonging to the defendant had been provided to me without any reference to his identity or any specific attack, my twenty-plus years of experience with terrorism, and the analysis of Jihadism in particular, would have immediately led me to the conclusion that these documents belong to an individual who identifies himself with the Global Jihadist Movement and who uses its ideology to justify terrorist violence.

The thousands of pages of jihadist documents supplied to me by the US Attorney's Office represent a very extensive collection of key authors and works central to the Jihadist Movement. More important, the documents authored by the defendant himself, as well as the images, videos and audio tracks in his possession, provide first-hand evidence of his self-identification with the Jihadist Movement, with its objectives, and with the violent means for achieving these goals.

Since 9/11—and even before—there have been numerous attempts to identify the key ingredients of the radicalization process that lead to Jihadist violence. Despite the existence of important works such as Marc Sageman's *Understanding Terror Networks*[29] and the contribution made to the discussion by the NYPD report, *Radicalization in the West: the Homegrown Threat*,[30] there is no one pattern to how a non-violent individual becomes a member of the Jihadist Movement willing to execute terrorist acts.

In the case of the Tsarnaevs, one can point to geopolitical events that may have contributed to the process of radicalization, or at least accelerated it, such as the success of Islamist forces in Syria or the renewed fighting between Israel and Hamas, but the only tangible similarity between this incident and other acts of jihadist violence is the ideology shared by the perpetrators, the narrative of an Islam infected by Western influence and a loss of faith; the oppression of Muslims; the need to re-establish a theocratic system of governance; and action to punish the infidels and destroy their un-Islamic systems.

The narrative written in the boat where the defendant was apprehended after the bombing cannot be read in any way but as the testimony of an individual who has knowingly participated in terrorist acts because he subscribes to the ideology of Global Jihad and wishes to kill for this cause and so receive eternal rewards.

According to the documents provided and written by the defendant, his progress toward the religiously justified use of terrorist violence was not rapid or sudden but the result of several years of radicalization. This is supported by the open sentiments expressed in several of the high school papers he wrote.

Beginning with the defendant's brief untitled essay for his honors world literature course, he describes a family history shaped by the need to leave Russia as a result of the putative persecution and violence meted out by the government against the Tsarnaev family for being Chechen Muslims—violence which in his world literature 2. essay he refers to as a "genocide" comparable to the Holocaust.

The defendant is very clear in his essay entitled *A New Journey* that his identity is that of being a Chechen, a people he typifies as being brave "fighters." He tells of his anger at the cowardice of the Chechen relative he was living with after having moved to the US For the defendant, Chechens are "spartans" who are "undefeatable," typified by Tsarnaev's grandfather who fought the Russians and whom he calls a hero in his student questionnaire. In the same questionnaire he is adamant: "I am not an American."

Then in his two papers on the book *Ask Me No Questions* by Marina Budhos, the defendant agrees with and amplifies the argument that the events of September 11, 2001, led to a "dehumanization" of Muslim immigrants in the US and the broader Muslim world, and in his essay *The Predator War*, he calls the US use of drones "basically murder" which could spark a "rebellious movement."

Together these sentiments can be considered as the foundation for the beliefs that fed the defendant's radicalization, his move to violent acts of terrorism, which culminated in Tsarnaev's justification and explanation of his actions as provided in the narrative left in his hand in the boat where he was captured.

In that written evidence, the defendant is explicit in his praise and admiration for his brother who, through his violent acts in the preceding days, has achieved the highest level of heaven.

All the defendant says he is praying for now is for "Allah to make me a shahied" (sic), since his brother, who is now dead, has been rewarded with being amongst the most righteous in paradise, thanks to his status as a martyr to the faith.

Reprising the theme of persecution and genocide from his high school essays on the Chechen Muslims of Russia, the defendant accuses the US government of "killing our innocent civilians." The defendant writes that as a Muslim he must respond in kind because that is "how Muhammad wanted it to be." The Holy Warriors, the mujahideen must awaken, "fighting men who look into the barrel of your gun and see heaven."

There is no doubt in the tone, or qualification of his approval of his brother's terrorist acts and his desire to emulate them.

ASPECTS OF THE CASE RELEVANT TO THE SENTENCING PHASE

The Boston Marathon bombing represents a quintessentially Jihadist operation.

Although the narrative of the Jihadist Movement is one in which alleged oppression must be responded to by an elite class of warrior, those that chose to be mujahedeen or soldiers of Allah, the actions thus initiated do not lead to any form of conventional mode of warfare.

The nation-state members of the international system, America included, have no issue with recruiting, or even conscripting, young men and women to be soldiers risking their lives on the battlefield. Yet, when they do so, these individuals are bound by the international laws of war, as based upon the Hague and Geneva Conventions and Protocols which regulate armed conflict. The Global Jihadist Movement utterly rejects these requirements and limitations on the use of force and instead focuses on methods of attack and target-selection philosophies which aim to achieve the exact opposite of what the laws of war were intended to do, such as regulate the use of force and minimize non-combatant civilian casualties.

From S. K. Malik's text *The Quranic Concept of War* to the first issue of the al-Qaeda magazine *Inspire*, with its instructions for how to turn a pressure cooker into an IED and maximize injuries by including extra shrapnel and placing the device in crowded public areas, the Jihadist Movement has encouraged the targeting of helpless men, women, and children, be they office workers in downtown Manhattan on 9/11, civilian commuters on British mass-transit on 7/7, or marathon runners on Boylston Street. In doing so, the Jihadist Movement follows an age-old tactic. Since it cannot directly defeat the un-Islamic state it ultimately wishes to destroy, it targets those members of its society that are unprotected and so generates fear amongst the broader population and thereby increases the pressure upon the political elite to acquiesce. This double dynamic of terrorist targeting can be represented visually as:

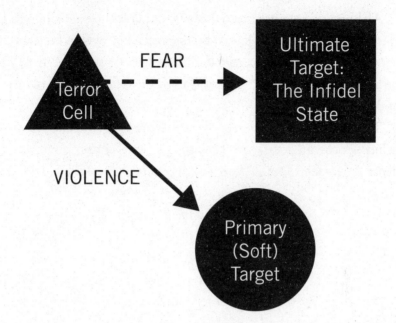

The objective of the terror attack is therefore to sow as great a fear as possible through the general population by using means that are wholly unpredictable, unregulated by the laws of war, and which engender a lack of trust in the capacity of the state to protect its citizens.

The more civilians that can be killed, maimed, or psychologically damaged for life, the more successful the Jihadi operation has been. A mass amateur sporting event in a major city fits this requirement perfectly. At the same time, should the operation lead to the deaths of the perpetrators, that is in fact also a positive result, since the Jihadist narrative guarantees salvation and eternal rewards for the martyred mujahedeen.

Dzhokhar Tsarnaev consumed a wealth of extremist material produced and propagated by the. This movement has as its objective the destruction of un-Islamic systems and the establishment of a theocratic caliphate. Its methodology calls for terrorist attacks against non-Muslims and provides extensive details on how to execute attacks which maximize civilian casualties.

Through his writings and actions, the defendant demonstrated not only a sympathy for the movement and its objectives, but a willingness to act as a "soldier of Allah" and kill or hurt as many people as possible in the hope of being rewarded as a martyr to Islam.

Why Jefferson Really Had a Koran and What He and Adams Thought about Islam

When Keith Ellison, America's first Muslim congressman, was sworn into office in 2007, the Fake News media made much of his having taken the oath on a copy of the Koran that belonged to Thomas Jefferson. The message was that we could all learn a lesson in broadmindedness from our multicultural third president.

Nothing could be farther from the truth.

Jefferson acquired a Koran to understand the Jihadi enemy our new nation faced in the form of the Barbary Pirates. He and his fellow Founding Father John Adams offered an assessment of that enemy in the following report to Secretary of State John Jay. And remember: He who can falsify the past owns your future.

American Commissioners to John Jay
   Grosr. Square March 28th. 1786

Sir,

Soon after the arrival of Mr. J. in London, we had a conference with the Ambassador of Tripoli, at his House.

The amount of all the information we can obtain from him was that a perpetual peace was in all respects the most advisable, because a temporary treaty would leave room for increasing demands upon every renewal of it, and a stipulation for annual payments would be liable to failures of performance which would renew the war, repeat the negotiations and continually augment the claims of his nation and the difference of expence would by no means be adequate to the inconvenience, since 12,500 Guineas to his Constituents with 10 pr. Cent upon that sum for himself, must be paid if the treaty was made for only one year.

That 30,000 Guineas for his Employers and £3,000 for himself were the lowest terms upon which a perpetual peace could be made and that this must be paid in Cash on the delivery of the treaty signed by his sovereign, that no kind of Merchandizes could be accepted.

That Tunis would treat upon the same terms, but he could not answer for Algiers or Morocco.

We took the liberty to make some inquiries concerning the Grounds of their pretentions to make war upon Nations who had done them no Injury, and observed that we considered all mankind as our friends who had done us no wrong, nor had given us any provocation.

The Ambassador answered us that it was founded on the Laws of their Profit [sic], that it was written in their Koran, that all nations who should not have acknowledged their authority were sinners, that it was their right and duty to make war upon them wherever they could be found, and to make slaves of all they could take as Prisoners, and that every Musselman who should be slain in battle was sure to go to Paradise.

That it was a law that the first who boarded an Enemy's Vessell should have one slave, more than his share with the rest, which operated as an incentive to the most desperate Valour and Enterprise, that it was the Practice of their Corsairs to bear down upon a ship, for each sailor to take a dagger in each hand and another in his mouth, and leap on board, which so terrified their Enemies that very few ever stood against them, that he verily believed the Devil assisted his Countrymen, for they were almost always successful. We took time to consider and promised an answer, but we can give him no other, than that the demands exceed our Expectations, and that of Congress, so much that we can proceed no further without fresh instructions.

There is but one possible way that we know of to procure the money, if Congress should authorize us to go to the necessary expence, and that is to borrow it in Holland. We are not certain it can be had there. But if Congress should order us to make the best terms we can with Tunis, Tripoli, Algiers and Morocco, and to procure this money wherever we can find it, upon terms like those of the last loan in Holland, our best endeavours shall be used to remove this formidable obstacle out of the way of the prosperity of the United States.

Inclosed is a Copy of a Letter from P. R. Randall Esqr. at Barcelona, the last from Mr. Barclay was dated Bayonne. It is hoped we shall soon have news from Algiers and Morocco, and we wish it may not be made more disagreeable than this from Tunis and Tripoli. We are &c.

John Adams

Thomas Jefferson

Notes

CHAPTER 2

1. You can listen to the original audio of President Truman's declaration at http://www.americanrhetoric.com/speeches/harrystrumantrumandoctrine.html.

AMERICA'S WARRIORS: CHESTY PULLER

1. He had, in fact, already attended officer candidate school in 1919, and he had been commissioned in the reserves five years before shipping out to Haiti. Because of the reduction in strength of the corps after World War I, however, his officer rank was inactive, and he remained a corporal until returning to the mainland.

2. To this day, marines on basic training can be heard intoning the cry "Chesty Puller never quit!" when tried to their limit and beyond.

3. Jon T. Hoffman: "Battle for Henderson Field," *World War II*, November 2002.

AMERICA'S WARRIORS: EUGENE "RED" MCDANIEL

1. This account is a summary of the full story found in Captain McDaniel's autobiography (written with the assistance of James L. Johnson), *Scars & Stripes: The True Story of One Man's Courage in Facing Death as a Vietnam POW* (Nashville: Broadman Press, 1975). I am honored to have met Captain McDaniel and treasure the signed and dedicated copy of his book that he gave me.

2. This method is strikingly similar to the one my father suffered in the basement of the communist secret police headquarters in Budapest, although he was bound with wire rather than rope. The human body has been the same anatomically for millennia, thus it is unsurprising that torture methods have evolved little over time.

3. *Scars & Stripes*, op. cit.

4. Column 1, Row 1, stood for the letter A, along the way to 5/5 for Z. In this way the abbreviation for the Viet Cong, VC, could be conveyed by tapping five times, followed by a pause, then one tap, followed by one tap, pause, and then three more.

5. *Scars & Stripes*, pp. 15–16.

6. Incredibly, the North Vietnamese didn't even confirm that McDaniel was alive until 1970, three years after he had been captured.

CHAPTER 4

1. For the story of how the Global Jihadi Movement was built and the ideological evolution of its key strategists and theologians, see my previous book, *Defeating Jihad: The Winnable War*, especial chapter four, "The Enemy Masterminds: The Grand Strategists of Modern Jihad."
2. National Commission on Terrorist Attacks upon the United States, *The 9/11 Commission Report*, July 22, 2004, p. 172.

AMERICA'S WARRIORS: WHITTAKER CHAMBERS

1. Chambers' given name was Jay Vivian, but he was known as Whittaker, his mother's maiden name.
2. The following chronology is based in part on the excellent introductory lecture "Whittaker Chambers' Witness for the Twenty-first Century" by Dr. Greg Forster, posted by the Acton Institute: https://www.youtube.com/watch?v=mNlTigcvcpM .
3. Whittaker Chambers: *Witness*, Regnery History, originally published in 1952.
4. To this day there are those who insist on Hiss's innocence, even though the ultra-secret Venona intercepts, since declassified, clearly show that he was not only a secret communist but an agent of Stalin and the Soviets.
5. C-SPAN still has many video links of the original HUAC footage, starting with this one of Hiss's denial and Chambers' response: https://www.c-span.org/video/?79536-1/hiss-chambers-hearing
6. In 1984, Whittaker Chambers was posthumously awarded the Presidential Medal of Freedom by President Ronald Reagan for his contribution to "the century's epic struggle between freedom and totalitarianism."

CHAPTER 5

1. And for the complete catalogue of Dave's excellent interviews, go to: https://www.rubinreport.com
2. Turning Point USA is an incredibly worthy national organization run by the indefatigable Charlie Kirk which promotes the message of limited government and free market on America's college campus. Please check them out at https://www.tpusa.com and support them if you are able.
3. For the full video see the *Rubin Report* video published on YouTube, April 27, 2018, https://www.youtube.com/watch?v=Y2cXHmSjDO0
4. Dave Rubin: "Why I Left the Left," Prager University https://www.youtube.com/watch?v=hiVQ8vrGA_8&vl=en
5. "Obama's Scrub of Muslim Terms under Question; common links in attacks," Rowan Scarborough, Washington Times, April 25, 2013 https://www.washingtontimes.com/news/2013/apr/25/obamas-cleansing-of-islamic-terms-suppresses-commo/
6. Dave Rubin: "Why I Left the Left," Prager University, https://www.youtube.com/watch?v=hiVQ8vrGA_8&vl=en
7. http://www.sds-1960s.org/PrairieFire-reprint.pdf
8. The National Security Strategy of the United States of America, The White House, December 2017 https://www.whitehouse.gov/wp-content/uploads/2017/12/NSS-Final-12-18-2017-0905.pdf
9. President Trump's Speech to the Arab Islamic American Summit https://www.youtube.com/watch?v=4RipNA1mOac

APPENDIX TWO: WHO ARE THE JIHADIS?

1. See Sebastian Gorka: "Understanding History's Seven Stages of Jihad," *CTC Sentinel*, Vol. 2. No. 10, Oct. 3, 2009, Combating Terrorism Center at West Point, available at: https://

www.ctc.usma.edu/posts/understanding-history's-seven-stages-of-jihad.

2. For full details see Thomas Joscelyn: *The Muslim Brotherhood: Understanding it Roots and Impact*, Foundation for Defense of Democracies, undated.

3. The title is sometimes translated as *Signposts Along the Way*. www.kalamullah.com/Books/Milestones%20Special%20 Edition.pdf.

4. See Albert j. Bergesen, ed., *The Sayyid Qutb Reader* (New York: Routledge, 2008).

5. Yaroslav Trofimov: *The Siege of Mecca: The 1979 Uprising at Islam's Holiest Shrine, and the Birth of al Qaeda*, Doubleday, 2007.

6. Op. cit.

7. Lawrence Wright: *The Looming Tower: Al-Qaeda and the Road to 9/11* (New York: Knopf, 2006).

8. http://www.religioscope.com/info/doc/jihad/azzam_defence_1_table.htm.

9. https://www.yumpu.com/pt/document/view/7647367/malik-quranic-concept-of-war

10. For a detailed, and perhaps the best, explanation of al *wara al barra* see Stephen Ulph's "Islamism and Totalitarianism: the Challenge of Comparison" in Katharine Gorka and Patrick Sookhdeo, eds., *Fighting the Ideological War: from Communism to Islamism* (McLean, Va.: Westminster Institute, 2012).

11. See the terrorist tradecraft sections of the al Qaeda magazine *Inspire* detailed below.

12. See the discussion of the video and audio *nasheeds* (Islamic chants) found in the possession of the Defendant and discussed below, especially: *When will the Muslim Ummah Unite?*

13. Jihadist nasheed: *When will the Muslim Ummah Unite?* Details below.
14. *Inspire*, Summer 2010, p. 2.
15. *Inspire* magazine, Summer 2010, p. 5.
16. *Inspire* magazine, Summer 2010, pp. 8–10 and p. 11.
17. *Inspire* magazine, Summer 2010, p. 31.
18. *Inspire* magazine, Summer 2010, p.33-41.
19. *Inspire* magazine, Summer 2010, p.40.
20. *Inspire* magazine, Summer 2010, p.56-58.
21. *Inspire* magazine, Summer 2010, p.58.
22. *Inspire* magazine, Summer 2010, p.58.
23. *U.S. v. Mustafa, Kamel Mustafa et al.*
24. *U.S. v. Al Timimi*, 04-CR-385.
25. https://www.youtube.com/watch?v=bmX-Wbyo99A.
26. National Consortium for the Study of Terrorism and Responses to Terrorism (*START*), University of Maryland. See http://www.start.umd.edu/tops/terrorist_organization_profile.asp?id=4357
27. *START*, op. cit.
28. https://www.youtube.com/watch?v=CvrRLsXE5RI.
29. Marc Sageman: *Understanding Terror Networks*, University of Pennsylvania Press, 2004.
30. M. D. Silber and Arvin Bhatt: *Radicalization in the West: the Homegrown Threat*, NYPD Intelligence Division, 2007.

INDEX